THE UNIVERSITY OF
WINCHESTER

Martial Rose Library
Tel: 01962 827306

To be returned on or before the day marked above, subject to recall.

Shakespeare

Shakespeare Now!

Series edited by Ewan Fernie and Simon Palfrey
Web editors: Theodora Papadopoulou and William McKenzie

Visit the *Shakespeare Now!* Blog at http://shakespearenowseries
.blogspot.com/ for further news and updates on the series.

SHAKESPEARE NOW!

Tragic Cognition in Shakespeare's *Othello*

Beyond the Neural Sublime

PAUL CEFALU

Bloomsbury Arden Shakespeare
An imprint of Bloomsbury Publishing Plc

B L O O M S B U R Y

LONDON • NEW DELHI • NEW YORK • SYDNEY

Bloomsbury Arden Shakespeare

An imprint of Bloomsbury Publishing Plc

Imprint previously known as Arden Shakespeare

50 Bedford Square	1385 Broadway
London	New York
WC1B 3DP	NY 10018
UK	USA

www.bloomsbury.com

BLOOMSBURY, THE ARDEN SHAKESPEARE and the Diana logo are trademarks of Bloomsbury Publishing Plc

First published 2015

© Paul Cefalu, 2015

Paul Cefalu has asserted his right under the Copyright, Designs and Patents Act, 1988, to be identified as author of this work.

British Library Cataloguing-in-Publication Data
A catalogue record for this book is available from the British Library.

ISBN: PB: 978-1-4725-2346-4
ePDF: 978-1-4725-3318-0
ePub: 978-1-4725-2192-7

Library of Congress Cataloging-in-Publication Data
A catalog record for this book is available from the Library of Congress.

Series: Shakespeare Now!

Typeset by Fakenham Prepress Solutions, Fakenham, Norfolk NR21 8NN
Printed and bound in India

CONTENTS

ACKNOWLEDGEMENTS

This book owes much to the incisive commentary and encouragement that I received from Ewan Fernie and Simon Palfrey. I thank them both for the care with which they read several versions of the manuscript. The editorial and production team at Bloomsbury, especially Margaret Bartley, Emily Hockley, Claire Cooper and Kim Storry, have been exceptionally helpful in bringing the manuscript to publication.

Several ideas for the argument of the book were formed during conversations that I had with participants of the 2013 Shakespeare Association of America seminar 'Shakespeare and Consciousness', as well as members of the 2013 Renaissance Society of America seminar on cognition and affect. I thank, in particular, Hannah C. Wojciehowski and Clifford Werier for their valuable insights on cognitive approaches to Shakespearean drama.

At Lafayette College, members of the Academic Research Committee, as well as my colleague Joseph Shieber, deserve special mention for their overall support of this project.

Portions of the book evolved out of my essay entitled 'The Burdens of Mindreading in Shakespeare's *Othello*: A Cognitive and Psychoanalytic Approach to Iago's Theory of Mind', copyright © 2013 Folger Shakespeare Library. This article was first published in *Shakespeare Quarterly* 64.3 (2013), 265–94. Reprinted with permission by Johns Hopkins University Press.

GENERAL EDITORS' PREFACE TO THE SECOND-WAVE OF THE SERIES

We begin with the passions of the critic as they are forged and explored in Shakespeare. These books speak directly from that fundamental experience of losing and remaking yourself in art. This does not imply, necessarily, a lonely existentialism; the story of a self is always bound up in other stories, shared tales of nations or faiths or of families large and small. But such stories are also always singular, irreducible to the generalities by which they are typically explained. Here, then, is where literary experience stops pretending to provide institutionalized objectivity, and starts to tell its own story.

Shakespeare Now! is a rallying cry, above all for aesthetic immediacy. It favours a model of aesthetic knowledge as *encounter*, where the encounter brings its own, often surprising contextualizing imperatives. Implicit in this is the premise that art is as much a subject as an object, less like aggregated facts and more like a fascinating person or persons. And encountering the plays as such is unavoidably personal.

Much recent scholarship has been devoted to Shakespeare *then* – to producing more information about the presumed moment of their inception. But this moment of inception is in truth happening over and over, again and again, anywhere that Shakespeare is being experienced anew or freshly. For the fact is that he remains, by a country mile, the most important *contemporary* writer – the most performed and read, the most written about, but also the most remembered. But it is not a question merely of Shakespeare in the present, as though his vitality is best measured by his passing relevance to great events. It is about his works' abiding *presence*.

In some ways criticism needs to get younger – to recover the freshness of aesthetic experience, and so in part better to remember why any of us should care. We need a new directness, written responses to the plays which attest to the life we find in them and the life they find in us.

Ewan Fernie and Simon Palfrey

INTRODUCTION

What is it Like to be Iago? Cognition and the Explanatory Gap

When the philosopher Thomas Nagel influentially challenged us to imagine 'what is it like to be a bat?' he was promoting the idea that consciousness or subjective experience is not reducible to the material or biophysical substrates of cognitive science.[1] No amount of knowledge regarding the functional or intentional states of bats, nor technical understanding of the bat's sonar or echolocation, would capture the unique experience of *being* a bat, the 'something that it is like' to perceive the world in the manner of that winged and shrieking creature.

The elusive bat has heavily influenced what philosophers now describe as the 'explanatory gap' concerning the relationship between cognitive processing, on the one hand, and consciousness and phenomenality, on the other. According to the foundational assumptions of cognitive science, the brain relies on internal representations and computations, many of which are subpersonal and inaccessible to personal awareness, in order to process information. Because this naturalist and materialist approach to cognition describes how the brain works, it tends to neglect comparable assessments of how one feels or perceives when cognizing. An intractable 'mind–mind' problem seems to have been created at the price of attempting to resolve the 'mind–body' problem: once we naturalize the mind (dispensing once and for all with the idealizing tendencies of Cartesian dualism), we are left with bridging the gap between the cognitive/computational and the conscious/ phenomenological mind.

Philosophers and cognitive scientists have been working dutifully to resolve the explanatory gap and so-called 'hard problem' of consciousness.[2] The belief that consciousness is extraneous or irrelevant to cognition is often called 'conscious inessentialism', which itself branches into forms of eliminativism and epiphenomenalism: while cognitive processes might give rise to subjective experience, such processes do not causally depend on consciousness.[3] Yet philosophers, well known for their thought experiments, often raise the 'zombie' objection to inessentialism: surely we can imagine creatures with cognitive abilities that are functionally equivalent to our own, creatures who move throughout the world as we do, but who do not feel or experience it in a comparable manner. Such thought experiments suggest to the 'new mysterians' that consciousness is an integral part of human sentience, no doubt based in the material substrate of our brain, but that we are not constituted to understand its nature.[4] The most ambitious attempt to integrate cognition and consciousness has come from those who take an embodied–enactive approach: instead of viewing the mind as a disembodied black box of representations, information and rule-governed operations (all of which are sequestered from the environment), this more dynamic approach assumes that the mind is a self-organizing system, cognition an exercise of 'skillful know-how' in situated contexts.[5] Whether or not such situated approaches have solved the problem of consciousness, they have helped close the explanatory gap between phenomenality and subpersonal cognition by embedding subjectivity in the context-sensitive, emotional and sensorimotor realms of the cognitive unconscious.

I will have more to say about situated cognition later, but for now I would ask those engaged by Shakespearean drama and literary criticism generally to shift from imagining 'what it is like to be a bat' to imagining 'what it would be like to be Iago' (no doubt a disturbing prospect, but not an unfathomable shift in perspective for those who would demonize both the creature and the character in *Othello*). I would ask further that those sceptics who question whether we should ascribe psychological realism to literary characters suspend for a moment their suspicions regarding character criticism. The Romantic school converged in the opinion that, as Samuel Taylor Coleridge remarked, if Iago is indeed 'passionless', he is also 'all will in intellect'.[6] William Hazlitt found in Iago a 'diseased intellectual activity', a 'complete abstraction of the intellectual from the moral being'.[7] A. C. Bradley held that, if Iago is 'destitute of humanity', and displays a 'deadness of feeling' emotionally, he reveals 'remarkable powers of intellect and will, his ingenuity and versatility in sorting out "unforeseen opportunities" unparalleled among dramatic characters'.[8] It was up to G. Wilson Knight to establish more clearly the dualism that was implied by the Romantics: against the concrete, radiant beauty of Othello and Desdemona, Iago represents a 'critical, intellectual' cynicism that is 'formless, colourless', without a 'visual reality'.[9] All of this suggests that, against or beneath the positivity of Iago's exquisite cognitive abilities, we find a hollow emotional make-up, not only absent of fellow-feeling, but devoid of the very forms of consciousness that would make him (and his motives) understandable. Even his amoralism and malice, Hazlitt reminds us, are not *personal*, but *intellectual*.[10]

What is Iago if not an embodiment of the explanatory gap between cognition and consciousness? We are drawn to Iago because we understand (perhaps envy) his cognitive acumen, his ability to manage the intentional stance so well, to read and act so effectively on the perceived beliefs and desires of his peers.[11] To a certain extent, we all rely on such 'theory of mind' (ToM) attributions, and Iago seems sublimely cognitive in his ability to infer and draw out such theories about the disparate behavioural patterns of Othello, Dedemona, Roderigo and Cassio. And to a limited extent, Iago also extends his cognition *via* external agents such as Roderigo. But if we have a keen sense of what it is like *to think* like Iago, it doesn't follow that we have a keen sense of what it is like *to be* Iago. We have difficulty in imagining the latter not because Iago is unimaginatively bad, or that we can't (or shouldn't) project consciousness on to a literary character, but rather because Iago's cognitive capacities are so overmastering, rendering him victim to what I describe as his hypermindedness, that any forms of phenomenal consciousness seem to be submerged under such cognitive bloat.

The case of Iago asks us to imagine what would happen to our sense of ourselves as phenomenally conscious, perceiving subjects, if our subpersonal cognitive nonconsciousness became too manifestly conscious. ToM, like so many cognitive processes, is largely a habitual process carried out imperceptibly, but in Iago's case it seems to have become so obsessively conscious that it leads to his discontentment. When we can imagine what it would be like to fixate on those aspects of cognition that ordinarily lie between conscious and nonconscious experience, then we have at least begun to experience what it is like to be Iago.

This is not to say, as is too often the case in criticism of Iago, that he is a character who is unable to feel or perceptually experience anything robust or meaningful. He is clearly beset with envy, and emerges as the least contented character in Shakespeare's play, 'contentment' and its various cognates being a recurring term in the text, variously associated with tranquillity, self-fulfilment and invulnerability (to stay with Shakespeare's own idiom). Recent debates in the philosophy of mind can help us provide a more fine-grained context in which to describe Iago's discontentment. According to the terms of the 'cognitive phenomenology' debate, on a traditional view of intentionality, cognitive states of believing, desiring and judging do not have an experiential or 'raw feel':

Bodily sensations and perceptual experiences are prime examples of states for which there is something it is like to be in them. They have a phenomenological feel ... Cognitive states are prime examples of states for which there is not something it is like to be in them, of states that lack a phenomenology.[12]

But according to the more recent, liberal position, intentional states do indeed have a phenomenal character, 'and this phenomenal character is precisely the what-it-is-like of experiencing a specific propositional attitude'.[13] I believe that Iago exemplifies the liberal side of the debate, the side that views the phenomenological realm as extending beyond the sensory realm. The designation 'cognitive' rather than 'sensory' phenomenology will help us to approach what it is like to be Iago, and in doing so will help us to rethink Iago's relationship to empathy, in particular. Once we appreciate the implications of 'cognitive empathy' (as set against the more commonplace view of embodied or situated empathy), we will not find it counter-intuitive to say that Iago is one of the most empathetic characters in the play.

We might say, following Alan Richardson and others, that because Iago reveals or allegorizes a 'brain's-eye' view of cognition, he (and we as spectators) uncannily encounter the 'neural sublime'.[14] Drawing on images of the naked or voided brain in Keats and Shelley, Richardson suggests that the Romantic neural sublime, unlike the Kantian sublime, is fundamentally a material sublime through which we intuit not the idealized, transcendent supersensible self, but the physiological neural mechanisms working beneath our perceptual illusions.[15] Analogous to the ecological sublime – described by Christopher Hitt as Henry David Thoreau's manner of achieving transcendence with nature as such – the neural sublime exalts the brain itself, 'which grows strange, awesome, and of titanic proportions in relation to the conscious subject, overwhelming it and yet leaving it with a sense of what Wordsworth calls "possible sublimity".'[16] The phenomenon of the neural sublime seems to be legitimized by some of the recent findings of neuroscience, particularly the ways in which the brain creates the illusory world that the mind perceives. Experiments on motion-blindness, for example (which reveal that, when tracking motion in a picture, we ordinarily fail to see objects that are otherwise salient), imply that the conscious mind is provided with simulacra constructed by the brain, usually in order to provide efficient, offloaded processes of cognition. Such perceptual illusions abound – we all have visual blind spots in our retinal field because of the placement of our optic nerves, though we do not usually see such blind spots – suggesting for Richardson the awesome, sublime power of the brain that we can perceive only at moments of rupture or breakdown. The neural sublime would have us imagine that the 'brain itself expands to cosmic proportions and figuratively swallows the universe', or, in Emily Dickinson's words, 'the brain is wider than the sky'.[17]

I suspect that for every person who would celebrate such a brain's-eye view of the world, there is a person for whom such a view is a constraining, neuroreductive blind alley. And many in this latter camp would no doubt find themselves vulnerable when confronted with the systematic reduction of selfhood or subjectivity to material, neuronal substrates, the sort of reductivism that for some cognitivists leads to an egoless or epiphenomenal sense of selfhood and perceptual consciousness. The argument of this book is that Iago is a *neuro-reactionary* character: his well-known egotism and solipsism stand as a fragile bulwark against an assailing cognitive unconscious; he is a character for whom the neural sublime is so constricting that he stages, through the route of masochism and the eventual toppling of Othello, his own death.

My argument is, as Edward Pechter would say, unashamedly Iagocentric, but Othello too gets a hearing, if only as a foil to Iago's embattled cognitions.[18] Where Iago is tragically mindful, Othello is pathetically mindblind. Both characters additionally seem to extend their cognitions, akin to Andy

Clark and David Chalmers' well-known example of Otto, a victim of Alzheimer's disease, whose memory is enhanced through his notebook entries, whose very mind gets extended to such a cognitive prosthesis.[19] But in extending his mind Iago is at least superficially a bigger loser than Othello. I will argue that, for several reasons, Iago's offloading of his cognitive schemes to his several dupes paradoxically heightens, rather than eases, his excessive mind-reading or ToM hyperattunement. Othello seems much worse off for allowing his mind to extend through Iago: Iago serves Othello more like a computer with a deadly virus than like a cognitively enhancing notebook. But to enlist Iago as his cognitive agent has the potential to provide the seemingly obtuse Othello with an ethical release. In what measure does Iago serve as Othello's cognitive extension? If that extent is significant, and Othello's mind is in some sense Iago's, then how can we hold Othello accountable?

Cognitive theory has the virtue of enabling us to reconstruct the manner in which literary characters like Iago or Othello think, but because it typically takes as its subject an ideally rational agent, it cannot meaningfully determine why such characters think the way that they do. Blakey Vermeule argues convincingly that literary characters intellectually stimulate us because they provide 'social information' and the 'deep truth about people's intentions'.[20] Yet I suspect that cognitive theory alone cannot provide such 'deep' intentional truths, or even that the tracking of 'intentionality' as understood by cognitive theory can provide such ontological, if not epistemological access.[21] Dorrit Cohn is right to point out that fiction is uniquely suited to suggest the 'privacy of a character's consciousness', but this is the other side of the explanatory gap that cognitive literary theory alone cannot explore.[22]

Perhaps the leading theoretical and methodological candidate for providing such supplementary insight into a character's 'consciousness' is phenomenology: through a rigorous observance of the subjective experience of intentional objects, phenomenology can peel away the biases of interpretation and reveal basic facts of consciousness. Yet as Paul Ricoeur and others have argued, phenomenology is primarily a reflective and descriptive analysis, and often relies too heavily on first-person reports, many of which are biased or simply incorrect.[23] We will not understand Iago if we subscribe to what Daniel Dennett calls 'lone-wolf autophenomenology', in which we just take at face value his first-person reports; heterophenomenology, in which we bracket Iago's reports on how he thinks and feels, subjecting them to the rigours of rational, third-person scrutiny (as any good literary critic will ordinarily do), is a better starting point, although it will not get us far enough in reconstructing the underlying reasons motivating those reports.[24]

I will be suggesting that, given the ways in which Iago complexly *works through* what I describe as his cognitive handicaps, themselves symptoms of his underlying sense of being ontologically overwhelmed by Othello, the most robust supplement to a cognitive approach to his character is a psychoanalytic one. Psychoanalysis can help us to understand why Iago seems to victimize himself through his very plot against Othello, as if the entire scheme is not only sadistic but masochistic, revealing a death drive that resolves in his cryptic silences by the close of the drama. If cognitive theory, particularly notions of theory of mind and extended cognition, provides us with opening critical gambits with which to evaluate Iago's inimitable mentalizing, the very manner in which those cognitive abilities are pathologized in the play points us to the prescriptive, rather than just descriptive explanations that depth psychology can provide. When Iago cannily subverts Othello, he is perhaps less cannily working out resolutions to his own discontentment. What follows is an argument for an integration of cognitive and psychoanalytic criticism. My guiding belief is that, while the former is better equipped phylogenetically to explain *how* characters think, the latter is better equipped ontogenetically to explain *why*, in their embedded story worlds, particular characters think the way that they do.[25]

I would emphasize that my approach aims to supplement rather than dismiss the cognitive approach. With respect to understanding the genuinely tragic dimensions of the play, the cognitive approach is valuable, if only because, as I will argue, the *telos* of Iago's character is to orchestrate a purgation of the cognitive. 'What you know, you know' (5.2.304): Iago's refusal to elaborate, to justify, to show insight into his crimes, has led more than one critic to conclude that Iago's unexpiated guilt occludes catharsis.[26] Iago's silence suggests 'reverse anagnorisis' for Edward Pechter, or 'destruction without catharsis' for Richard Raatzsch.[27] But the catharsis for Iago is identifiable with that very destructiveness, if by destruction we mean not simply the literal torture and death that awaits him, but the destruction of the very cognitive overload that renders him discontented throughout the play.

I hope to show that Iago is a character who, for most of Shakespeare's play, is pathetic for not being able to internalize the therapeutic advice (most typically Stoic precepts) that he vouchsafes to Roderigo and Othello. As critics have long noted, despite playing the role of therapist, Iago is much less apathetic, content and reasonable than he lets on. His ultimate achievement, though, through the very negation of cognitive hypermindedness, is at least the momentary fantasy of contentless thought, a window into the perversely desired *boredom* of Stoicism, as Hegel would have it.[28] But it is Schopenhauer who is Iago's philosopher, for Iago's turning of his will away from life, his contraction of the world as (cognitive) representation into an absolute ego, his resigned approach toward death, his heroic escape from the neural sublime, all provide him with the tragic catharsis that, I will be arguing, is unachievable for us. And such catharsis is out of our reach precisely because Iago comes near to closing the explanatory gap between cognition and consciousness that for us will no doubt remain inexplicably open.

CHAPTER ONE

The Limits of Mind-reading, or how Iago Gives the Lie to Cognition I

There is a long tradition among Shakespeare scholars of attributing canny psychological powers to Iago. For A. C. Bradley, Iago's most remarkable gift is his insight into human nature, a gift that, according to Stephen Greenblatt, manifests as improvisational power, the 'role-player's ability to imagine his nonexistence so that he can exist for another and as another'.[1] Iago's evil seems to lie in his talent for what cognitive theorists would describe as mind-reading, the relative ability to access imaginatively another's mental world and, in Iago's case, cruelly to manipulate that world. Inversely proportional to Iago's mind-reading ability would be the mindblindness or at least metacognitive deficits of Othello, who seems too obtuse and closed off from others to fathom Iago's unimaginable designs.[2]

Cognitive theorists and evolutionary psychologists tell us that mind-reading or having a robust ToM confers natural fitness: to plumb the intentions of others is to be able to detect cheaters, manipulate truth-telling and track the past actions and predict the future behaviour of those around us.[3] But what if thinking too much about what others are thinking strikes at our very sense of contentment, an elusive quality that the play itself ascribes not to Iago but to Othello (at least before Iago's fabulations take hold)? Contentment is a perishable commodity that confers on us peace of mind to the degree that we are not bothered too much to mind the business of others; it is akin to a private and uninterrupted mode of attention that our New Age psychologists would call psychic flow.[4] What if, despite our marvelling at Iago's terrific intuitive powers (and his own blustering rationalizations aside), his adept mind-reading is a psychological handicap?

Such an approach to understanding Iago's character involves rethinking the causal nexus among cruelty, motive and character in the play. Iago's evildoing does not follow from his mind-reading but gradually displaces it, which in turn provides him (in theory, if not in practice), with the contentment of which he is constitutionally bereft. The ontological gain of Iago's negation of his hyperattunement to others is the construction of his own self-narrative, a shift of attention from other to self that involves some sadomasochism along the way (with an emphasis on masochism). Cognitively overloaded, Iago is as much the victim as he is the exploiter of the imagined intentions and beliefs of those around him, his hyperbolic mind-reading not a manipulable talent as much as the unavoidable cause of his seemingly motiveless evil.

As I have previously remarked, the stubborn case of Iago reflects both the virtues and limitations of the new cognitive style of literary criticism, and the extent to which a psycho-analytic approach to understanding character can be gainfully, if surprisingly, allied with cognitive literary criticism. ToM provides us with an opening critical gambit with which to evaluate not only Iago's multilevel, recursive intentionality (impressively, he can keep several layers of third-person intentionality in his mind at once), but also the extent to which his overmentalizing belies a parallel first-person ToM aberration: Iago's obsessive tracking of other minds has much to do with his inability to adequately track his own mind, since third-person attributions of intentions are generally held to be modelled on first-person attributions. Yet I will argue that the way in which Iago works through this underlying problem with self-attribution is more understandable from the perspective of philosophical and psychoanalytic accounts of masochism. If cognitive theory has the advantage of explaining Iago's strange mentalizing by weighing it against normative cognitivist assumptions about ToM attunement, psychoanalytic theory has the virtue of explaining Iago's bid at resolving that problem without making recourse to a neurodevelopmental model the technical, physiological discourse of which is too remote from the folk psychological language of the play.[5]

Iago's servitude to cruelty

On the face of it, Iago does seem to be a talented and complacent mind-reader. Not only does the success of his project rest on his belief in Othello's 'free and open nature too / That thinks men honest that but seems to be so' (1.3.397–8), but he also intuits Roderigo's gullibility (and so easily convinces him of Desdemona's fickleness). He capitalizes on Desdemona's purity – 'For 'tis most easy / The inclining Desdemona to subdue, / In any honest suit' (2.3.330–1). The reach of Iago's evil is partly contingent on the predictive accuracy of his estimation of the characters of those about him: the dull honesty of Othello, the pliancy of Desdemona, and Cassio's 'rash' and 'choler'-filled nature (2.1.267), which he knows will respond violently to Roderigo's incitements.

Yet these characterizations are so reductive as to be types or caricatures, which is what Hazlitt was getting at in his much-cited remark in 1817 that Iago is 'an amateur of tragedy in real life', one who, as a portrait of Shakespeare himself, 'plays the role of playwright in scripting a plot, staging scenes and illusions, and bringing the drama to a tragic conclusion'.[6] Iago is indeed a playwright, but we grant him oversubtle talents when we compare him to Shakespeare. Iago does not conjure anything more than stock types in his own play. The distance between Iago and Shakespeare is measured in the generic language that Iago uses to characterize Othello from the outset. Consider critics' favourite Iagoism, the 'free and open nature' of Othello. In various locutions, these attributes are repeated throughout the play and attached to a complement of characters, not simply to Othello. Iago tells Cassio that Desdemona is 'so free ... a disposition' (2.3.311), and then underscores the point in his monologue, describing her as 'fram'd as fruitful / As the free elements' and 'inclining' toward 'any honest suit' (2.3.332–3, 331–2). Cassio thinks it 'freely' when he refers to Iago's insistence that Desdemona loves him. Iago describes his own advice as free and open – as if parodying everyone's erroneous opinion of his own honesty, as well as his very overuse of these terms.

The irony is that we embrace Iago's caricatured version of Othello when we see the latter as a hopeless innocent and gull. If Othello were so easily duped, why would he demand veridical evidence of Desdemona's infidelity? In his diatribe against critics such as A. C. Bradley, who seemed to senti-mentalize Othello by exalting Iago's unrivalled power to bring down such a great-souled man, F. R. Leavis reminded us of Othello's noble egotism and heroic self-dramatization, represented by the Moor's pompous diction, his belief that 'big wars' '[make] ambition virtue' (3.3.355–6) and his sense of Desdemona as a trophy wife. His love of her stems from self-centredness and is mingled with pride, sensual posses-siveness, a 'love of loving'.[7] Leavis concludes that a 'habit of self-approving self-dramatization is an essential element of Othello's make-up, and remains so at the very end'.[8]

Iago's dilemma lies between theory and practice. He has the unrelenting inclination, even ethos, for mind-reading, but he cannot easily or accurately do so in practice (improvisation is certainly one of his manifest talents, but his very need for it belies his inability predictively to gauge how his projects will unfold). His challenge is the inescapable, generic problem of

other minds, a challenge which in the world of the play trans-
mutes into a curse. Iago's outsider status derives from thinking
too much about what others are thinking, from never being
in the moment. The play has its own notion for this malady:
discontentment. When Iago foments Othello's jealousy, he
strikes at Othello's enviable sense of contentment, the latter's
most valued and self-proclaimed quality, variously described
in the play as self-satisfaction, ease, invulnerability or self-
fulfilment. Here is Othello's swan song to the unperturbed life:

> Farewell the tranquil mind; farewell content:
> Farewell the plumed troop, and the big wars,
> That makes ambition virtue: O farewell,
> Farewell the neighing steed, and the shrill trump,
> The spirit-stirring drum, the ear-piercing fife;
> The royal banner, and all quality,
> Pride, pomp, and circumstance of glorious war!
> And, O ye mortal engines, whose wide throats
> The immortal Jove's great clamour counterfeit;
> Farewell, Othello's occupation's gone!
>
> (3.3.354–63)

This is when Othello realizes that his world has been withdrawn
from him. In Stanley Cavell's description of Antony in *Antony
and Cleopatra*, 'Everything known to him as the world
recedes.'[9] Loss of contentment follows when his precious
self-narrative, his *telos* and 'occupation' as a self-possessed
soldier, loses meaning. This helps to uncover one of Iago's
principal motives that has been overlooked by critics, namely,
his constitutional *discontentedness* before he has even settled
on his stratagems:

> For that I do suspect the lustful Moor
> Hath leap'd into my seat, the thought whereof
> Doth like a poisonous mineral gnaw my inwards,
> And nothing can, nor shall content my soul,

Till I am even with him, wife, for wife:
Or failing so, yet that I put the Moor,
At least, into a jealousy so strong,
That judgment cannot cure.

(2.1.290–7)

Critics have frequently compared the fractured or compromised ontology of Iago to the fullness of Othello's being: Iago has been described as self-divided, empty, a forlorn nobody, while Othello seems, at least in the early scenes, to be unified, solid, a veritable somebody. Janet Adelman remarks that

Othello – and particularly in relation to Desdemona – becomes Iago's primary target in part because Othello has the presence, the fullness of being, that Iago lacks. Othello is everywhere associated with the kind of interior solidity and wholeness that stands as a reproach to Iago's interior emptiness and fragmentation.[10]

Such a critical view approaches an important ontological divide between the two characters but is articulated in residual postmodern jargon. Just what does it mean to claim that one character or person is 'empty' or another is 'full', and how do these terms converge with discontentment? Fullness, for example, aligns more closely in the play with honesty and naiveté, as when Roderigo denies the charges of fickleness and libidinousness that Iago levels at Desdemona: 'I cannot believe that in her, she's full of most blest condition' (2.1.247–8).

Contentment as defined in the play has much to do with the cognitive aspects of the mind-reading–mindblindness continuum. To be absolutely content is to be entirely secure and invulnerable, qualities inversely proportional to jealousy, as Othello quickly intuits. As Iago comments:

Poor and content is rich, and rich enough,
But riches, fineless, is as poor as winter

To him that ever fears he shall be poor:
Good God, the souls of all my tribe defend
From jealousy!

(3.3.176–80)

And what aspect of jealousy in particular strikes at peace of mind? Othello provides an answer: 'Exchange me for a goat / When I shall turn the business of my soul / To such exsufflicate and blown surmises' (3.3.184–6). To be rendered jealous but uncertainly so; to be overcome with surmises about the genuine feelings and motives of others not only toward oneself, but toward a third party: these are the preoccupations that force one to unravel and predict another's intentions and actions. About mind-reading, Jesse Bering concludes that 'people "cannot turn off their mind-reading skills even if they want to. All human actions are forevermore perceived to be the products of unobservable mental states, and every behaviour, therefore, is subject to intense socio-cognitive scrutiny".'[11] At what point, though, does obsessive behavioural and intentional scrutiny become a psychological handicap? The threshold in the play that separates discontentment from mind-reading is as thin as the fabric of a handkerchief or the veil of a foredoomed Desdemona.

Recall Othello's exclamation upon seeing Desdemona once he returns from war:

It gives me wonder great as my content
To see you here before me ...
My soul hath her content so absolute,
That not another comfort, like to this
Succeeds in unknown fate.

(2.1.183–4, 191–3)

Contentment is the calmness that follows the duplicitous stratagems and competitiveness of war; contentment is silence, the hard-won pause in Othello's inflated rhetoric designed to impress and cover over his soldierly imprecision with words; contentment is attunement to the unspoken rhythms Othello now enjoys with Desdemona, those 'well tuned' reveries for which Iago will 'set down the pegs' (2.1.200), displacing quietude with mindful noise. 'Practising' upon Othello's 'peace and quiet' is simply to fill Othello's head with disconcerting ideas. This isn't primarily (or even necessarily) a process of self-alienation, fracturing or deconstructive loss of selfhood (whatever those heavy terms might mean); it is, less complicatedly, a process of making Othello too involved in the secret lives of others. And this ranges from the minimally attentive, for example, Iago's ability, through Montano, to begin to see beneath the prized virtue of Cassio to the latter's drunkenness – 'It were well / The general were put in mind of it' (2.3.124–5) to the maximally attentive, the cuckolding itself.

The source of Iago's discontentment is the motive for his evil. Just what is that source? Much of Iago's perturbations stem from envy, even paranoia, directed at Othello, Cassio and Desdemona. Yet to ascribe discontentment to envy or paranoia is to mistake a symptom for a cause. What leads to such uneasiness and thence to envy is his consuming tracking of others, as if he is discomposed by the very process of mindfulness rather than by any particular content or intentional object. Consider his comments to Roderigo on Cassio's character:

a knave very voluble, no farther conscionable than in putting on the mere form of civil and humane seeming, for the better compassing of his salt and hidden affections: a subtle slippery knave, a finder out of occasions; that has an eye can stamp and counterfeit the true advantages ... (2.1.236–42).

Of course, the occasion for this invective is to prompt Roderigo's gall against Cassio. But this is also a continuation of Iago's opening monologue in which he ruminates on the undeserved promotion of Cassio, that prattling arithmetician who, if only in Iago's mind, is a scheming opportunist whose every action belies a hidden intention to be ferreted out. Iago's vexation is not even paranoia, since these are perceived qualities in Cassio that, if realized, would affect Othello (and Roderigo), rather than Iago himself.[12] Drawing on theories of altruism and the evolution of cooperation, William Flesch has recently suggested that readers like narrative fiction because the heroes are typically strong reciprocators: they are adept at tracking villains and free riders and punish wrongdoers at significant cost to themselves.[13] Iago has all of the traits of a strong reciprocator except that he uses these traits for non-cooperative pursuits, the personal gains of which are not readily apparent.

Consider Iago's cogitations on the doubleness and secret aspirations of Othello and Desdemona: 'It cannot be that Desdemona should long continue her love unto the Moor … put money in thy purse … nor he to her. … These Moors are changeable in their wills … When she is sated with his body, she will find the error of her choice' (1.3.342–52). Not only is there no evidence on which to base either of these predictions, but Iago is consumed by his predictive accuracy regarding Desdemona's nature in particular, and later embellishes on the theme. After adducing Othello's limitations, including his defective manners and approaching age, Iago predicts: 'Now, for want of these requir'd conveniences, her delicate tenderness will find itself abus'd, begin to heave the gorge, disrelish and abhor the Moor, very nature will instruct her to it, and compel her to some second choice' (2.1.229–34).

Iago formulates plausible theories about his peers' behaviour – theories based partly on intuition, partly on past experience and tracking such actions – but such theories seem to spin quickly out of control. It is one thing to recognize that Cassio puts his manners to good effect, but another to surmise that he is an immoral timeserver; one thing to assume that Desdemona might long for a younger man, but another to posit that she will eventually abhor Othello and cuckold him. Not only does Iago embellish too much his theories about others, but he firmly believes such theories to stem from something natural about people, their 'second natures' over which they have no control. One way of describing this sensitivity to the pathologies of others is to call Iago a cynic, as does G. Wilson Knight. Knight comments about Iago's disbelief in the continued love of Othello and Desdemona: 'He is cynicism loathing beauty, refusing to all its existence. Hence the venom of his plot: the plot is Iago – both are ultimate, causeless, self-begotten. Iago is cynicism incarnate and projected into action.'[14] But this attributes yet another worldview to Iago, an identity and way of organizing his perceptions that offers him the stable self and peace of mind that he envies in others.

Iago's mind-reading and fine attunement typically work him up into a hostile, vengeful state; these abilities do not provide any measure of uncomplicated pleasure (more on his masochism later). While Iago expects the worst in people and is intuitively attentive to their hidden selves, his expectations have two results: they become so exaggerated as to be counter-intuitive, and they unsettle him and make him hyper-vigilant. Iago swears to exact revenge on Othello because he just 'knows' that he has been cuckolded; his frenzied ire against women is guided by his acute (mis)perception of their practised infidelity. Iago's mantra, 'I am not what I am' (1.1.65), is an antidote to a much more corrosive, if unspoken and disturbing, belief – that people are not what they seem to be.

Iago's case legitimizes an influential criticism of ToM, namely, the claim made by simulation theorists that people do not routinely spin theories of other minds, theories that are based on anticipated behaviour and tacit algorithms or rules of acting. David Premack and Guy Woodruff underscored the theoretical component of ToM in their original conceptualization: 'A system of inferences of this kind is properly viewed as a theory, first, because such states are not directly observable, and second, because the system can be used to make predictions, specifically about the behaviour of other organisms.'[15] If ToM marginalizes the role of empathy in cognitive tracking (for Premack and Woodruff, empathy is restricted to the perceived purpose of a target, and is not linked to inferences about another's knowledge), simulation theorists reject the 'theory' component of extrapolating from unobservables and argue instead that people re-enact third-party behaviour based on the contents of their own minds: 'Ordinary people', Alvin Goldman remarks, 'fix their targets' mental states by trying to replicate or emulate them.'[16] Iago's mind-reading is an exaggerated version of ToM: nothing of what he predicts of others is based on extrapolations from his own mind, that is, of mental simulations that typically follow first-order empathy or simply putting oneself in another's place. As if he were a ToM zombie, Iago is controlled almost wholly by his predictive knowledge of others.[17]

But this begs the question of why Iago would persist in the very mind-reading practices that, despite appearances, unsettle him. Here, cognitive literary criticism provides a clarifying response. The prevailing view of why we enjoy fiction is that it provides not passive pleasure, but pleasure yielded from 'intellectual workouts', in Lisa Zunshine's term, from teasing and testing our ToM capabilities in order to provide us with the confidence that our mental modules are running efficiently. 'It is possible, then,' Zunshine notes, 'that certain cultural artifacts, such as novels, test the functioning of our cognitive adaptations for mind-reading while keeping us pleasantly aware that the "test" is proceeding quite smoothly.'[18] Reading narratives is a mode of 'cognitive *play*' that, as Brian Boyd points out, renders art and narrative adaptive, in that stories are 'designed to engage human *attention* through their appeal to our preference for inferentially rich and therefore *patterned* information' (art is thankfully not what Steven Pinker has called intellectual 'auditory cheesecake' or a mere by-product of natural selection).[19] The pleasure we gain from tracking multiple levels of intentionality among fictional characters is like the boost we experience from scoring highly on an intelligence test. But Zunshine provides an important caveat: the pride and pleasure that cognitive tracking affords readers can become exasperating because we are inclined to treat fictional *personae* as real people. We over-speculate about the states of mind of fictional characters (beyond what the author has suggested) and lose the sense of cognitive mastery that fiction provides as an escape from our messy, intention-laden social world:

> Our Theory of Mind allows us to make sense of fictional characters by investing them with an inexhaustible repertoire of states of mind, but the price that this arrangement may extract from us is that we begin to feel that fictional people do indeed have an inexhaustible repertoire of states of mind.[20]

Recall that Hazlitt and subsequent critics typically describe Iago as a stand-in for Shakespeare, his entire plot akin to a script (however faulty) written by a playwright. Extend the analogy a bit: as playwright and reader of his own narrative, Iago, methodologically tracking his characters' intentions and actions through the creation of complex patterns of behaviour with nuances he is privileged to understand, can test and theoretically plume himself on his ToM prowess. And to some extent, he proves himself to be cognitively adept. But we have also seen that his interpretations of others' intentions are as disconcerting as they are gratifying. He creates the circumstances under which he can test his ToM capabilities but fails to process the behavioural and intentional results of those tests (A. C. Bradley shrewdly remarked that Iago could not even stop the plot once it was underway).[21]

How do we explain the persistence of Iago's overmentalizing, despite the psychic costs? ToM is usually described as a domain-specific, inferential adaptive ability. As part of our cognitive 'adaptive unconscious', it typically works for us without our having consciously to put its other-regarding energy into motion.[22] Iago's incessant tracking of, and then obsessive ruminating on others' hidden plans, suggests a wholly non-inferential application of ToM, as if his overmentalizing were due to some other cognitive impairment. An apt analogy is to the pathology of obsessive-compulsive disorder, as it is understood by evolutionary psychologists: avoiding germs is an otherwise self-preserving trait that becomes a handicap in the too-conscious rituals of the obsessive hand-washer.[23] What might fuel Iago's overblown mentalizing to such an extent that his very indulgence of it causes as much cognitive dissonance as it does gratification?

One recurring idea in cognitive studies is that people have as little direct awareness of their own minds as they do the minds of others. Since many of us are anti-Cartesians, we would probably agree that unmediated private access is an illusion, but what makes private access counter-intuitive is the assumption that, just as we can only model theories of other minds, so we can only fashion theories of our own minds, that a deficit in third-person ascriptions would signal a corresponding deficit in first-person attributions: 'Even though we seem to perceive our own mental states directly, this direct perception is an illusion. In fact, our knowledge of ourselves, like our knowledge of others, is the result of a theory.'[24] The implication of this bi-directional ToM is that we can only make inferences about our own minds by turning a ToM spotlight inward. Peter Carruthers offers the most recent formulation of what he describes as an 'interpretive sensory-access theory': 'Our access to our own propositional attitudes is almost always interpretive (and often confabulatory), utilizing the same kinds of inferences (and many of the same sorts of data) that are employed when attributing attitudes to other people.'[25] A deficit in third-person mentalizing will entail comparable deficits in self-awareness. The aetiology of autism is frequently invoked as an example of such dual-processing impairments:

> The logical extension of the Theory of Mind deficit account of autism is that individuals with autism may know as little about their own minds as about the minds of other people. This is not to say that these individuals lack mental states,

but that in an important sense they are unable to reflect on their mental states.[26]

To what extent can we extrapolate a cognitive impairment in self-awareness from Iago's hypermindedness? We have seen that his exaggerated mind-reading often misleads and disconcerts him, and that rational intuitions about others turn into tortuous theories. ToM would predict that he suffers similar problems of self-attribution, that despite his frequent pronouncements of the multi-layered complexity of his ego ('I am not what I am'), such overestimations are confabulated theories about himself (as if he were as uncertain about his own motives as about his peers' intentions). I believe that this is the case, and that our cognitivist speculations should direct us back to the text in order to test our supposition about Iago's theory of his own mind, this time with a focus on his manifest cruelty and the manner in which his cuckolding plot not only provides him with a missing self-narrative, but also has as its endpoint the very contentment that his mind-reading places out of his reach.

Putting cruelty first

What separates Iago's discontentment from Othello's eventual discontentment is that, while Othello's is responsive, Iago's is constitutional. But how does cruelty, in particular, serve Iago's purposes to unsettle Othello and, in that insidious process, find the satisfaction that I am suggesting a degree of mindblindness affords? Acts of cruelty do not merely elicit a range of responses, some anticipated, from the victim. Nor do they simply draw out latent aspects of the victim's personality (in this case, Othello's own penchant for envy and rage, despite his frankness). Cruelty manufactures a space for an improvisational dialogue between agent and victim. The tortured victim who asks, 'Why are you doing this to me?' is forced to inhabit the heads of those whose conduct he suspects (and so formulate some theory of the other's mind).[27] Othello's equanimity is lost when he is forced to turn his attention to the motives of Cassio, Desdemona and, eventually, Iago.

Another way of saying this is that Othello becomes discontented when he is compelled to leave the comforts of his relative mindblindness. This is a process of losing the self in the other. Conversely, in his cruelty, Iago finds a small measure of satisfaction because that cruelty provides him with a compensatory self-narrative, and a belief system that in turn provides him with a theory of his own mind. Cruelty is the means by which he finds value in himself, and cruelty creates a safe distance between himself and Othello. Such distance results in the negation of the very mindedness that drives the process in the first place. Cruelty toward others projects the agent's mind on to the victim (as the victim attempts to explain why he is being victimized), but the agent can in turn theorize about his own mentalizing by getting inside the victim's head: cruel agents can study their own intentions by reading the narrative effects of their actions on the victim.

Consider that there is no direct correlation between Iago's knowledge of others and his knowledge of himself. By 'knowing' I mean simply having a confident sense of how one's self or another will act based on guiding perceptions of one's own or another's patterns of thinking and behaviour. That Iago doesn't clearly know why he hates Othello is some evidence that he does not read himself as well as he does others. While all of Iago's motives for hating Othello (plain greed, being passed over for the lieutenancy, believing he has been cuckolded) have been questioned by the play's best critics, it is worth looking at some of Iago's most revealing comments regarding this hatred:

> I hate the Moor,
> And it is thought abroad, that 'twixt my sheets
> He's done my office; I know not if't be true ...

Yet I, for mere suspicion in that kind,
Will do, as if for surety.

(1.3.384–8)

Iago's suspiciousness of the truth of such claims makes him seem less naively trusting than Othello, but his leap from suspiciousness to certain belief is irrational. Is this not the kind of epistemological leap one would make if one didn't trust oneself, didn't quite know one's own motives for hating someone else? That Iago does not reflect any more trenchantly on why he has such a motive, or which motive is the decisive one, suggests that he remains opaque to himself despite his talent for knowing others, and that the problem of other minds is both an intrasubjective and intersubjective one.

That Iago acts cruelly in the play needs no special elaboration. Soon after the plotting has begun, he relishes in the pleasures of cuckolding Othello: 'Let us be communicative in our revenge against him: if thou canst cuckold him, thou doest thyself a pleasure, and me a sport' (1.3.367–9). Later, Iago marvels at his own mounting stratagems:

Make the Moor thank me, love me, and reward me,
For making him egregiously an ass,
And practising upon his peace and quiet,
Even to madness.

(2.1.303–5)

Whether or not we call him a sadist, Iago's pleasure in others' pain presupposes cruelty: it is no wonder that Verdi, in his variation on this theme in *Otello*, has Iago unashamedly announce: 'Credo in un Dio crudelis' (*I believe in a cruel God*).[28]

But does Iago's cruelty afford him any self-discoveries along the way? One thing Iago does learn is the nature of his own capacity for evil. Consider his musings on the devilish quality of his tactics:

And what's he then, that says I play the villain,
When this advice is free I give, and honest,
Probal to thinking, and indeed the course
To win the Moor again? For 'tis most easy
The inclining Desdemona to subdue,
In any honest suit ...
Even as her appetite shall play the god
With his weak function. How am I then a villain,
To counsel Cassio to this parallel course,
Directly to his good? Divinity of hell!

(2.3.327–32, 338–41)

It seems reductive to claim that Iago simply rationalizes here; more likely, he is reviewing his conduct and its effects, taking stock of the inclinations of his several dupes in order to gauge the reach of his evil and derive the source of it. He proves to himself not the fact of his villainy (that is never in question in his mind) but the full extent of his diabolical nature. A penchant for cruelty initiates the process, but his awareness of the bottomlessness of his own cruelty impels the process once under way. Cruelty is self-fulfilling, both the cause and result of his actions.

Iago learns something about his own mind through the process of exploiting other minds. Consider his last monologue:

I have rubb'd this young quat almost to the sense,
And he grows angry now: whether he kill Cassio,
Or Cassio him, or each do kill the other,
Every way makes my game ...
If Cassio do remain,
He has a daily beauty in his life,
That makes me ugly.

(5.1.11–14, 18–20)

This is a simple prediction based on his perception of Roderigo's anger; how things will unfold is unclear to Iago.

What is more important is what he realizes about himself in contrast to Cassio. Iago discovers about himself unintended consequences of his plot, as if his monitoring of others inescapably forces him to monitor himself, his mind-reading forcing upon him a measure of mindfulness that he adjusts by fine-tuning his tragedy, which in turn provides more self-information to continue the cycle. Exactly what Iago might learn about himself is beside the point. What he gains from the cruel acts toward Othello is a kind of alienation effect: the more Othello suffers, the less attuned Iago becomes, and so the distance between the two widens as the play unfolds. But, as we will see in the next chapter, both the motives for and consequences of that distancing are helpfully explained by the means of a psychoanalytic supplement to the cognitivist approach to understanding Iago's character.

CHAPTER TWO

From CBT/Stoic Therapy to Psychoanalysis and Masochism

We have begun to see that Iago's overmentalizing, a symptom of a theory of mind aberration at the level of third- and first-person attributions, gradually works to his own benefit. This is an example of a problem that serves as its own cure, at least to the extent that it provides him with a self-narrative, the very absence of which his mind-reading had been a symptom. And when we think about the complex psychic processes through which Iago attends to his attributional problems, the cognitive explanation yields to a psychoanalytic one. As a hypothesis of the way in which people inferentially fashion theories about the opaque notions of others and themselves, ToM can be interpretively productive. But it is not as hermeneutically valuable when assessing the ways in which, through fantasy and intersubjective engagement, fictional characters seem to construct their own therapies (often through disavowal). Nor is it as valuable when we ironically know more about such characters than they do and so, as readers and critics, reconstruct psychic processes that underlie manifest symptoms (arguably, the psychoanalytic critic, like the cognitive critic, likes to test his or her mental agility). And although we don't need to argue that Shakespeare invented the unconscious, the irreducibly dynamic sense of Shakespeare's characters warrants a psychoanalytic supplement to cognitive theorizing: 'What is interesting about Shakespeare's characters', Meredith Skura aptly remarks, 'is not their diseases but their movement through disease to some kind of curative reorganization. Their proper parallel is not the neurotic but the neurotic in analysis.'[1] It is precisely this allegorization of the reorganization of disease – think not just of Iago, but also of Leontes, Hamlet, perhaps Macbeth – that cognitive literary theory cannot yet track as compellingly as psychoanalytic theory.

Imagine extending the cognitive approach in order to account for the play's *working through* of Iago's pathology. Consistent with the protocols of diagnostic psychiatry, a cognitive explanation would tally Iago's symptoms and perhaps place him along the autism spectrum, with one subtle modification: autistics are held to have ToM deficits. Their low scores on false-belief tests represent their mindblindness, yet I have suggested that Iago overmentalizes. This would place him on an extreme end of the autism scale as an example of a high-functioning autistic who perhaps suffers from 'intense world syndrome'; on the pervasive developmental spectrum, these unfortunate individuals experience hyper- rather than hypoattunement: 'The lack of social interaction in autism may … not be because of deficits in the ability to process social and emotional cues, but because a sub-set of cues are overly intense, compulsively attended to, excessively processed and remembered with frightening clarity and intensity.'[2] Autistic people may, therefore, be neither mindblind nor lacking in empathy for others, but hyperaware of selected fragments of the mind. One can imagine making some such argument about Iago, if only because it helps to explain his obsessive but faulty mindfulness. But other cognitive personality disorders are equally explanatory: Iago may exemplify the traits of the trendy new personality disorder described as the 'dark triad' of '*Machiavellianism, narcissism,* and *psychopathy*', which, aptly, has been tied to very high scores on ToM tests but relatively low scores on emotional intelligence tests.[3] Or one might describe him as an overmentalizing paranoid schizophrenic (although I have already cautioned that paranoia is an etiological red herring when it comes to understanding Iago's hyperattunement).

The problem is that, given the dynamic nature of the psychic processes that Iago displays (his character's exemplification of Meredith Skura's 'neurotic in analysis'), such static cognitive diagnoses would lead to an interpretive dead end. How does one treat, according to the protocols of diagnostic psychiatry, some of the disorders described above? The usual strategy would be pharmacology supplemented by a cognitive behavioural regimen. Cognitive behavioural therapy assumes that, through mindful exercises – consciously turning irrational into rational beliefs – and aversive conditioning and habitual training, one can reconstruct one's cognitive architecture, a process that offers little in terms of a critical hermeneutic for understanding Iago's intractable self-deceptions.[4] The route to a fuller discussion of the limits of CBT to our understanding of a character like Iago is, perhaps surprisingly, Stoicism, to which we now briefly turn, after which we can provide the psychoanalytic supplement to the cognitivism that we've been tracking.

A stoic and CBT interlude

Stoicism provides a historical dimension to Iago's (and Othello's) ruminations on contentment that can help us further contextualize the manner in which Iago serves simultaneously as therapist to himself, and anti-therapist to Othello. Seneca and Plutarch are the two most prominent Stoics who wrote of *euthymia*, typically translated as contentment or tranquillity. Seneca provides advice to Serenus, a well-intentioned man who loses mental equanimity each time that he becomes aroused by the affairs of others – 'reading of high courage and goaded by examples of nobility', for example – but who longs to have his mind 'rooted in itself', involved in 'nothing external, nothing that requires an umpire'.[5] Seneca's tutelage is a compendium of the Stoic philosophy of good living. Acknowledging that we are constitutionally hyperminded – 'by nature the mind is active and prone to movement. It welcomes all opportunities for excitement and diversion'[6] – Seneca cautions against some of the more obvious threats to tranquillity, including putting too much stock in external goods, refusing to accept one's lot in life and meddling in the affairs of others. Tranquillity above all requires one to accept the unpredictability of Fortune, which prepares one's mind for reversals: 'He has no grounds for fearing her [Fortune], because he counts among transitory things not only his property and possessions and social standing but also his own body and his eyes and his hand and whatever else makes life particularly dear to a man, even his own self, and he lives as one who is on loan to himself and intends to return everything without complaint when the debt is recalled.'[7]

Contentment is neither achieved through social insularity nor a solipsistic withdrawal into oneself. It requires self-monitoring, a healthy mean between disengagement and sociality, open-mindedness and flexibility to change. The tranquil mind will be sufficiently attuned not simply to the intentions of others, but to the alterations of the external world, including the vicissitudes of nature, Fortune and God, so as not to be caught out when reversals do occur. Plutarch more specifically describes this anticipation of reversals and embracing of 'whatever turns up' as an antidote to complacency and sickness of the soul:

> It is our task, if we are wise, to accept in a suitable manner whatever accrues from Fortune and to assign to each event a place in which both what suits us shall help us most and what is unwanted shall do least harm. For those who are without skill and sense as to how they should live, like sick people whose bodies can endure neither heart nor cold, are elated by good fortune and depressed by adversity.[8]

There are moments in *Othello* when Iago directly echoes Stoic ideas about contentment. Recall his warning to Othello about the perils of fearing the loss of riches: 'Poor and content is rich, and rich enough, / But riches, fineless, is as poor as winter / To him that ever fears he shall be poor' (3.3.176–8). Compare this to Seneca's belief that secure poverty is more desirable than vulnerable opulence: 'We must therefore reflect how much easier to bear is the pain of not having money than that of losing it: and we will come to realize that the less opportunity for loss poverty provides, the less likely it is to torment us.'[9] Since he knows that his scheming will render Othello unable to internalize and maintain the Stoic wisdom, Iago's playing of the Senecan therapist to Othello might be seen as just one more turn of the screw. 'I see, sir, you are eaten up with passion' (3.3.397), Iago taunts Othello, who has just demanded proof of Desdemona's disloyalty. Yet, interestingly, Iago uses the generic and categorical 'passion' rather than isolates any psychic imbalance or humour of Othello's (choler, for example), suggesting that Iago does not merely put Othello to the test of his scheming, but puts the very theory of Stoic tranquillity to the test. What does it take to displace one's peace of mind with impassioned involvement, Iago seems to be asking, as if working on Othello is more a proximate means to an anti-Stoical end than an end unto itself (Coleridge's tag for Iago as *experimenter* is apt here).[10] Once having discomposed Othello, Iago then tests out (really mocks) an overly glib remedy: 'Patience I say, your mind perhaps may change' (3.3.459), pointing out the typical nature of our mutability and wavering orientations to the world, as well as the weakness of a remedy that would preach self-knowledge and patience. Othello unwittingly plays into the mock-Stoic cycle of diagnosis and curative regimen by claiming a Stoic resolve likened to the 'icy current, and compulsive course' (3.3.460–1) of the Pontic, and then by invoking the impassibility of 'marble heaven' (3.3.467), to which Iago pays sham, unwavering reverence: 'I am your own for ever' (3.3.486).

None of this, however, eases Iago's sense that he cannot put the Stoic wisdom to practice in his own life: 'And nothing can, nor shall *content* my soul, / Till I am even with him, wife, for wife' (italics mine, 2.1.293–4), he has already confessed in his first aside. It is one thing to observe his self-proclaimed discontentment, another to note that, alongside that admission, he echoes the very Stoic advice that would be the remedy for such agitation. Not being able to put the proper therapy into practice, only able to preach such advice ironically to someone for whom he serves as a veritable poisoner, renders him pathetic, if not poignant, which is enhanced when we consider the still more apt advice of Seneca that would seem to be lost on Iago, given his sense of being passed over for the lieutenancy: 'Even if others hold the front line and fate has placed you among the third row of soldiers, play your part where you stand with your voice, your encouragement, your example … The service of a good citizen is never without some use.'[11] Such seemingly sound and rational therapeutic advice is ready at hand, and Iago *knows as much,* but is unable to internalize the precepts.

As I will suggest in a moment, Iago's plot conduces to a much more complex form of psychoanalytic therapy because the rational–Stoic option is just too idealistic, resting as it does on a facile method of exercising rational control of one's passions that glides superficially over Iago's desires to have Othello construct a boundary separating the Moor from his ensign. Another way of saying this is that Iago's plot serves as idiosyncratic therapy given that implicit forms of cognitive-behavioural therapy are unavailing. How have we arrived back at CBT from classical Stoicism? Not surprisingly, cognitive theorists have begun to trace the origins of their discipline directly to Stoic theories of impassability. In *The Philosophy of Cognitive-Behavioural Therapy*, Donald Robertson reminds us that Albert Ellis, the founder of 'rational–emotive behaviour therapy', had asserted that 'much of the theory of REBT was derived from philosophy rather than psychology'.[12] For Ellis, a fundamental postulate of REBT and CBT – that people are affected not by 'outside things' or events, but by their 'perceptions, attitude or internalized sentences *about* outside things and events' – is derived from Roman Stoicism, particularly Epictetus' *Enchiridion*, which famously postulates that 'Men are disturbed not by things, but by the views which they take of them'.[13] Shakespeare, too (or his insightful avatar, Hamlet), gets enlisted in this recent literature on CBT and Stoicism as a prototypical cognitive-behavioural therapist, given his pithy advice: 'There is nothing either good or bad but thinking makes it so'.[14] It follows that, according to CBT, self-monitoring techniques (in which the patient is coached to replace negative 'autosuggestive' thoughts with positive ones) derive from Stoic assumptions that emotional well-being follows from a disciplined scrutiny of irrational beliefs. A. A. Long's summary of Stoic therapy is wholly embraced by cognitive theorists: 'Happiness and a praiseworthy life require us to monitor our mental selves at every waking moment, making them and nothing external or material responsible for all the goodness of badness we experience.'[15] In the words of Epictetus: 'Some things are up to us and others or not', or in the words of the Christianized Serenity Prayer of Alcoholics Anonymous: 'God grant me serenity to accept the things I cannot change'.[16]

Against both the behaviourist and psychoanalytic approaches – both of which refuse to 'accept a patient's description of his psychological processes at face value' – CBT is concerned primarily with conscious meanings that are culled from the person's 'reports of his ideas, feelings, and wishes'.[17] Through 'careful introspection and the reports of internal experiences', the patient is made aware that he or she might be harbouring erroneous or irrational 'automatic thoughts'. 'The challenge to psychotherapy', according to Aaron Beck's foundational text on CBT, 'is to offer the patient effective techniques for overcoming his blindspots, his blurred perceptions, and his self-deceptions.'[18] The process aims to be step-wise and eminently logical: one recognizes maladaptive ideation through reflective distancing, and then, through further self-scrutiny, conversation with the therapist and habitual thought-exercises, reinstates rational and adaptive self-statements regarding the original target.

Imagine Iago in consultation with a CB therapist. The therapist opens with the following (only slightly caricatured) presentation: 'Ok, Iago, you've said repeatedly that you "hate the Moor". I think that it is important for you to distance yourself from what has clearly become an automatic thought. Can you reconstruct the circumstances under which you repeat this mantra to yourself and others? I want you to practise some self-monitoring techniques.' Iago's response? Something evasive, or a string of over-determined explanations: 'He has leaped into my seat, I have been passed over for the lieutenancy, and I love Desdmona.' The therapist's further solicitation: 'Please try to be rational, Iago; do you have any evidence for these views, which seem to have become habitual, automatic thoughts?' Iago might play along, admitting that he has no real evidence, ocular proof unavailing; he might then deny that he really loves Desdemona, reminding the therapist that he is the consummate method actor, that *he is not what he is*. Undeterred, our analytic therapist soldiers on:

I beg to differ that you are not what you are: individuals generally are what they think they are. My advice to you – consider it a homework exercise – is to follow an A, B,C sequence each time that you see the Moor: Let's assume that A, the Activating Stimulus, is the approach of Othello, and C, the Conditioned Response, is your subvocal mantra, 'I hate the Moor'. B is the blank in your mind that gets you from A to C. What you have to do is fill in that blank each time you move from A to C in order to figure out what is causing your hatred of Othello. I'm betting that there is some ready-at-hand narrative or conscious ideation that runs parallel to your thought-content of hating the Moor, correct?[19]

Iago remains silent. The therapist needs to reorient his approach; he asks whether there is anything that Iago actually *likes* about the Moor. Iago prefers this line of questioning, and admits that he has always liked Othello's handkerchief;

then, refusing to play passively along, wryly asks, 'I wonder why?'. The therapist, sensing an ideological threat, quips: 'We are not Freudians here, Iago. Sometimes a handkerchief is just a handkerchief. Perhaps we are back to envy?'. This strikes a harmonious note and Iago admits that, if he is being honest, the only thing that he envies about the Moor is (or was) the Moor's easy contentment. The therapist finds this line encouraging: 'OK, but we need to determine what makes you discontented, Fill in the blanks, Iago. There must be some *judgement* of yours regarding Othello that makes you hostile and discontented.' Iago cannot isolate the cause, but, half-aware of the means of a resolution, remarks that, if he can disrupt Othello's tranquillity, somehow he can achieve his own satisfaction, even if, oddly enough, that means his own death. This suggests to the therapist a depressive etiology, so he redoubles his commitment to rational probing, assuring Iago that depression is caused by maladaptive cognitions, which in turn stem from self-blame. At this point Iago remarks that they've already been through the dreary business of maladaptive cognitions, at which the therapist again reminds him that his internalized statements are fuelled by blurred perceptions, this time arming himself with Epictetus: 'Men are not disturbed by things, but by the views which they take of them.' Iago, no longer willing to engage, but wanting to correct the therapist once and for all, plays Hamlet against Epictetus: 'In the words of someone I would have liked to have known, "there is nothing either good or bad but thinking makes it worse".' The therapist responds: 'I think you are misquoting Hamlet, Iago – "There is nothing either good or bad but thinking makes it so",' to which Iago, satisfied with his misquote, and depleted of further conversational energy, responds coolly: 'Demand me nothing. What you know, you know.'

And so it would go: The CB therapist attempting to get Iago to think rationally about his automatic thoughts, Iago concealing, averting, and rationalizing at every turn. Putting Iago in this abortive dialogue with a cognitive-behavioural therapist is my way of suggesting that we need to put him back on to the psychoanalytic couch. We will see that, whatever its limitations, the psychoanalytic process parallels, as so many critics have noted, the very structure in motion of a play such as *Othello*. And the movement from symptom to insight that is the goal of therapy is recapitulated in the plot line of the play itself. This does not mean that we will leave off cognitivism entirely: we will see that the emergence into consciousness of Iago's cognitive nonconscious functionally serves like a psychoanalytic symptom in that it stands in for his inability to find the ontological separation from Othello that his sadomasochistic plot has as its endpoint.

Masochism and the death drive

Iago's cruel behaviour has often been described as sadistic.[20] In keeping with Freud's notion of a 'radically sexualized will', David Pollard argues that Iago's 'behaviour is sadomasochistic. This is apparent in his paralleled relationships with Cassio, Desdemona and Othello. In each case, the tormented Iago – a "poisionous mineral" gnawing his innards – identifies with a victim and achieves pleasure from the recognizability of the pain he has caused.'[21] Sadism is reflected in Iago's scripting of the 'erotomania' of Desdemona, with whom Iago identifies 'through the fiction of Cassio's dream': 'The sadomasochistic implications are clear. Thereafter, the inventor of a feminine criminal self who has enjoyed forbidden pleasures – a self with which he has identified – Iago proceeds to devise the appropriate punishment.'[22]

Such interpretations of Iago's sadism omit extended discussions of his masochism even when noting the convertibility of the terms. Although Freud first posited sadism as primary, the terms and concepts imply one another throughout his work.[23] Not only is masochism sadism turned upon oneself, but sadism cannot afford its peculiar pleasures if the sadist cannot identify with the masochistic desires of the victim (hence, Lacan's dictum that 'sadism is merely the disavowal of masochism').[24] Masochists, according to Freud and Lacan, stage elaborate scenes in order to contrive separation from others who have nominal power over them: 'Like the fetishist, the masochist is in need of separation, and his solution is to orchestrate a scenario whereby it is his partner, acting as Other, who lays down the law.'[25] Although they seem to render themselves passive, they coax, even bully the other into establishing boundaries through the imposition of paternal law. Masochists are always pulling the strings, such actions eliciting anxiety (not simply pleasure) in the sadist who is pressed to establish punitive sanctions.[26] The quest for pain is not the primary motivation of the masochist: 'Though it is often thought that the masochist is in search of pain, this is not what is essential; pain is merely a sign that the Other has agreed to impose a condition, limit, toll, penance, or loss upon him.'[27]

To what extent might we describe Iago as a masochist, and what peculiar gains, especially with respect to his hypermind-edness, does masochism afford him? In what manner can the psychoanalytic interpretation be integrated with the cognitivist framing that we have put in place? To seize too quickly on Iago's hatred of Othello passes over the former's fantasy of desiring and imagining being desired by Othello: 'It is indeed Othello and not Desdemona', Robert Matz writes, 'who is the primary object of Iago's and Cassio's desire. *Othello*, as has frequently been noted, is a play in which everyone stands in for, or represents, someone else, and because the person who stands in for you may also take your place, this exchangeability makes highly fraught the erotic/political suits constantly pursued in *Othello*.'[28] This fungibility of desire is conveyed in Iago's invented dream in which he establishes a homosocial relationship between himself and Othello: 'In sleep I heard him say "Sweet Desdemona, / Let us be wary, let us hide our loves"' (3.3.425–6). That Iago and Desdemona are confused in Othello's mind is represented in the twinned rhetoric earlier used to describe the two characters: 'By the world, / I think my wife be honest, and think she is not, / I think that thou art just, and think thou art not' (3.3.389–91), the question of honesty projected away from Iago and toward Othello.

The thrill that Iago gets from working up Othello's passions against him most suggests Iago's masochism: Act 3, scene 3 traces the ascendance of Othello's anger, culminating in his threats to Iago, which allow Iago to play the victim. To Othello's demand for 'ocular proof', or else Iago 'hadst been better have been born a dog, / Than answer my wak'd wrath' (3.3.367–8), Iago petitions:

> O grace, O heaven defend me!
> Are you a man, Have you a soul or sense?
> God buy you, take mine office, – O wretched fool …
> To be direct and honest, is not safe.
>
> (3.3.379–81, 384)

At this point, Iago has not simply cruelly manipulated Othello; he has propped up Othello as a volatile threat to himself, his pleasure unmistakable. But the culminating masochistic moment occurs at the end of the scene, when Othello establishes himself as law to challenge the heavens: 'Now by yond marble heaven, / In the due reverence of a sacred vow, / I here engage my words' (3.3.467–9). In response, a kneeling Iago pledges to relinquish all self-agency and offer himself up to Othello's command:

> Witness that here Iago doth give up
> The excellency of his wit, hand, heart,
> To wrong'd Othello's service: let him command,
> And to obey shall be in me remorse,
> What bloody work so ever.
>
> (3.3.472–6)

Iago achieves the masochist's fantasy of having the other arbitrarily implement a law that sanctions a boundary between self and other.

Despite so much critical attention to the handkerchief as fetish object, critics have not linked that object to the very masochism it underwrites.[29] The distinguishing mark of masochism as opposed to sadism is, for Deleuze, at least, the masochist's primary disavowal and secondary attachment to fetish objects (the psychoanalytic presupposition is that 'perverse' subjects disavow castration anxiety, itself prompted by the failure of paternal law to allow for such subjects to separate from the other).[30] In Lacan's formulation: 'The masochist tries to bring something into being ... by which the Other's desire makes the law.'[31] Emilia notes that Iago has asked for the handkerchief a hundred times, presumably before Iago's script has been written, implying that Iago wants the 'gift' (3.3.443) from Othello that the latter has given to Desdemona. The handkerchief would serve to sever, not narrow the relationship between Iago and Othello, which assumes that what bothers Iago about Othello is not primarily the fear of being cuckolded; it is more basically Iago's perception of being ontologically overwhelmed by Othello.[32] The fetishized handkerchief is a Freudian/Lacanian object *avant la lettre*, described literally as a 'thing' [*das Ding*] (3.3.304), which creates a 'lack' (3.3.323) when lost and is used to wipe Cassio's 'beard' (3.3.446), fur and hair typically working similarly to allow disavowal. Iago's elaborate sadomasochistic fantasy, the cuckolding plot, becomes necessary because he is unable to secure the appropriate fetish object before his elaborate play gets under way.

What about Othello's treatment of Iago restricts Iago's bid for psychic autonomy? Othello inscribes Iago as a caricature, a one-dimensional instantiation of the virtues of honesty and patience, a caricature that does not seem to be its own desiring agent. Another way of saying this is that Iago has no biographical self, only the one contrived for him by Othello. It is this absence of self-narrative that makes Iago vulnerable to the hypervigilance that I ascribe to him. In a wonderful reading of Othello's vulnerability to love, Tzachi Zamir remarks that Othello's self-definition is determined by his willingness to serve; this self-conceptualization is a tool that is threatened by Desdemona, who loves Othello too naturally and non-instrumentally: 'The erotic mismatch in *Othello* consists of Desdemona's penetrating loving gaze as unbearable for Othello, since it brings out something that resists reduction to the instrumental, a reduction that is what he is about.'[33] Othello's recession from Desdemona's love has everything to do with her not loving merely his biographical, caricatured military identity, the only identity to which he is accustomed.

As an extension of Zamir's argument, we can say that Iago's case is an inversion of Othello's: it is the instrumentalized, biographical self, the self defined by service as Othello's honest and reliable Ancient, against which he rails and which ideally would have been displaced by something more authentic – namely, the very soldierly identity that he admires in Othello. Iago's tragedy is that Othello projects his own values of service on to Iago – Iago serves Othello well, just as Othello serves Venice well – without realizing the precise type of service to which Iago would have himself put. When Iago cryptically remarks 'I am not what I am', he is making more than a stock comment on being versus acting; he is suggesting that he is not what he is because he is or has been simply what Othello has dictated that he be. We need to see Iago's pride in his duplicitous life as a reaction formation, for example, when he confesses to Roderigo, 'In following him, I follow but myself. / Heaven is my judge, not I for love and duty, / But seeming so, for my peculiar end' (1.1.58–60). There is no evidence that, before having been passed over for the lieutenancy, he had been guilty of the dissembling that he now embraces and that he has just attributed to Cassio. Harold Bloom reminds us of the ontological profundity of Iago's having been passed over militarily: 'Othello was everything to Iago, because war was everything; passed over, Iago is nothing, and in warring against Othello, his war is against ontology.'[34] Yes, but what is left in the wake of that slight is not a zero-degree identity or 'nothing', but rather an identity constructed wholly out of the perceived excesses of everyone else.

So it is that the culminating moment of Iago's fantasy carried out masochistically is Othello's designation of him, finally, as 'lieutenant' – 'Now art thou my lieutenant' (3.3.485) – which is followed by Iago's avowal, 'I am your own for ever' (3.3.486). The Lacanian application here is surprisingly precise, given Lacan's use of soldierly language to explain the masochist's desire to be 'commanded' (*se faire commander*).[35] Yet why doesn't such a separation fantasy hold? Why would Iago not want to maintain this imagined lieutenancy for/with Othello, perhaps finding satisfaction in destroying Desdemona and Cassio, but not Othello himself, not the paternal figure/law that he has just installed? To answer these questions requires that we see Othello playing a dual, contradictory role for Iago. On the one hand, Iago sees Othello as an ontologically overwhelming figure from whom he needs to separate (Othello as subject and object of love, depicted in the eroticized language in which Iago becomes twinned with Desdemona herself, and whose overweening appreciation of Iago's honesty is repugnant to Iago). On the other hand, Othello serves as the figure who can provide the paternal law to achieve separation from this first figuration of Othello, who can provide a symbolic military identity that would serve to displace any other identity Othello might foist upon Iago. The difference here is between the real and ideal paternal figure, the latter erected in the place of the former through the route of Iago's masochistic fantasy. If critics are correct to note the homosexual undercurrent between Iago and Othello, the homophobic Iago, through masochism, can trade that homoerotic relationship for a homosocial one.

In order to function as the ideal figure of paternal law, however, that figure needs to serve dispassionately as a symbolically 'dead' father ('This symbolic Father, insofar as he signifies the Law, is clearly the dead Father'[36]). The dead father both enunciates the law and stands above it: if he becomes too invested, partial, or emotional, the masochist would find unsustainable the fantasy of separation that the disinterested paternal law provides, and so the entire masochistic edifice would begin to topple. What seems to happen to Iago is that, quickly following his appointment as Othello's 'lieutenant' in their joint revenge against Cassio and Desdemona, Othello unravels so abruptly, suffering two seizures, that his role as ideal father is compromised. This helps to explain Iago's hectoring of Othello for not being sufficiently masculine: 'I mock you? no, by heaven. / Would you would bear your fortunes like a man!' (4.1.60–1); and then, 'Good sir, be a man, / Think every bearded fellow that's but yok'd / May draw with you' (4.1.65–6). Iago clarifies that it is Othello's having been overcome with grief that represents his loss of manhood: 'Whilst you were here erewhile, mad with your grief – / A passion most unsuiting such a man – / Cassio came hither' (4.1.76–8); and then, 'Marry, patience, / Or I shall say you are all in all in spleen, / And nothing of a man' (4.1.87–9). Iago's taunts are obviously designed to rattle Othello; yet this strategy of overtly insulting Othello is far removed from Iago's preceding strategies of false compliment and a rhetoric of servitude. Iago has hypothesized all along that he could reduce Othello to a level of what he describes as 'savage madness', yet we can imagine that Iago himself is not fully prepared to appreciate the evidentiary results of his hypothesis: to bring Othello down in this precise way, to castrate Othello (for that is the way it is implicitly described) is to level the idealized figure that Iago's fantasy has just constructed.

Without standing in as paternal law, Iago's masochistic fantasy loses force, and he redoubles his sadism in the wake of effeminizing Othello. For example, once the handkerchief 'evidence' is offered, Othello, at Iago's prodding, decides to murder Desdemona, Iago providing the cruellest of means: 'Do it not with poison, strangle her in her bed, even the bed she hath contaminated' (4.1.203–4). But while masochism and sadism seem to cycle fluidly throughout the play, perhaps we have overlooked the extent to which, for Iago, sadism is really a precipitate of a more primary masochism, primary because, in keeping with Freud's late theorizations of masochism, it is linked to *thanatos* or the death drive. By the time he had written *Beyond the Pleasure Principle* (1919) and *The Ego and the Id* (1923), Freud had decided that 'primary masochism', a 'turning round of the instinct upon the subject's own ego … is a return to an earlier phase of the instinct's history, a regression'.[37] Such a regression is directed away from the pleasure principle and guided by an instinct to return to 'an earlier state of things', which Freud cautiously described as follows: 'The dominating tendency of mental life, and perhaps of nervous life in general, is the effort to reduce, to keep constant or to remove internal tension due to stimuli.'[38] These internal tensions were linked to Freud's under-theorized account of chemical tensions and biological processes, but might we not argue by analogy that it is Iago's overstimulated mentalizing that needs to be negated via masochism if the primordial, even mythical contentedness so valued in the play can be approached?[39] And is not this ever-receding peace of mind or cognitive stasis perversely linked with Iago's imminent censure and 'torture' (5.2.369), most probably death, that is represented in his eerie, Bartleby-like avowal of silence: 'Demand me nothing, what you know, you know, / From this time forth I never will speak word' (5.2.304–5).

A psychoanalytic interpretation of Iago's motives alerts us to his bid for contentment amid the very chaos that he introduces into the Venetian court. Because ToM helps us to see that Iago's seemingly canny inferential abilities belie his self-confabulations and discontentedness, it partly clarifies why and how he thinks the way that he does. But ToM provides only an interpretive starting point, since it points to but leaves unresolved Iago's motives for his mental ambush of Othello. Such motives masochistically alleviate his discontentedness by providing him with some semblance of a theory of his own mind. ToM helps us to see that Iago's obsessive mind-reading is a symptom of some other cognitive misfire that is better approached from a psychoanalytic vantage point.[40]

To sum up the way in which the cognitive approach mingles with, or even presupposes, the psychoanalytic: Iago's ToM tracking, which enables both his cruelty and his attunement to his own mind, helps him to separate from Othello (call this his sadism). However, the pleasures afforded by ToM tracking are simultaneous with its psychic pains (discontentment caused by overthinking), a necessary persistence if Iago is to achieve fully his separation fantasy and prop Othello up as threatening master over him (call this his masochism). ToM and masochism work toward the same end, with ToM a manifest symptom of the masochism operating beneath Iago's conscious awareness. It is as if Iago's masochistic fantasy has hijacked his capacity for ToM by bringing the latter too closely into contact with his conscious and non-inferential thinking.

The claim that Iago's ToM impairment emerges as a psychoanalytic symptom assumes from a strictly cognitivist view an unholy integration of the cognitive adaptive unconscious (sometimes described as the 'nonconscious') and the Freudian unconscious. Cognitivists explain that the adaptive unconscious is the seat of learned, automatic behaviour, a nonconscious filter that modulates the amount and type of sensory information that enters into conscious awareness. This sort of implicit learning, of which ToM is an example, affords us the ability unconsciously to shift gears while driving, or play a Bach fugue from memory. The adaptive consciousness is not repressed or topographically beneath consciousness as much as parallel with it, more the hyper-rational guardian angel of consciousness than the irrational usurper of our mental awareness: 'Cognitive models of nonconscious mentation depict the processes of attention, sensation, perception, memory, and related functions all interacting in a logical fashion. This picture stands in direct contrast to the Freudian notion of an irrational unconscious driven by an id.'[41] But while there may be sufficient empirical evidence supporting the executive role of an evolutionarily stable adaptive consciousness, there is no compelling evidence that proves that the Freudian unconscious, or a comparable site of repressed impulses, is little more than a folk-psychological construct. One eloquent cognitivist, after dismissing

Freud's account of the unconscious in favour of the adaptive nonconscious as 'myopia', gudgingly accepts that repression has a place somewhere in our cognitive makeup: 'This is not to deny that some thoughts are quite threatening and that people are sometimes motivated to avoid knowing them. Repression may not, however, be the most important reason why people do not have conscious access to thoughts, feeling, or motives.'[42]

Given this bogey of repression for cognitive theorists, might we not supplement, rather than displace, the Freudian unconscious with the adaptive nonconscious?[43] ToM, presumably a universal, adaptive, cognitive module, provides us with a hermeneutic tool with which to measure Iago's obsessive overthinking, but because this otherwise adaptively unconscious mechanism seems maladaptive for Iago (it loses its automatic nature) we look for something else that will explain his behaviour. Rather than function here as an interpretive *a priori* or cognitive presupposition, ToM, in its manifestation as Freudian symptom, serves more like the return of the repressed, a recurring 'slip-of-the-mind' that evokes, rather than displaces, whatever repressed impulses might guide Iago's intentions. What we find are not parallel conscious and unconscious interactions, but an underlying masochistic proclivity causing an offline process (Iago's ToM attunement) to overtake an online mode of thinking (Iago's brittle consciousness).

By attributing not one but two forms of unconsciousness to Iago, have I not transgressed the literary dictum that literary characters are not realistically drawn people but non-naturalistic functions in texts bounded by the constraints of genre?[44] Here, I think cognitivism has actually reopened the possibility of character criticism for both cognitive and psychoanalytic literary criticism.[45] Cognitivists have compellingly argued that we naturally focus our evolved sense- and inference-making abilities such as cognitive simulation and ToM on literary characters in the same manner that we train such abilities on the intentions of familiar or unfamiliar people. Noting the propensity to use literary characters to engage, test and modulate a range of our cognitive skills, Blakey Vermeule describes literary characters as 'the greatest practical-reasoning schemes ever invented', concluding that 'the reasons that we care about literary characters are finally not much different from the question of why we care about other people'.[46] For Alan Richardson, the identification of the literary and the naturalistic depends precisely on the extent to which characters represent ToM capabilities: 'Austen's *Emma* demonstrates that one of the ways to make a character's consciousness seem real or "plausible" is to represent that character putting his or her own theory of mind to work.'[47] Such characters acquire an even more heightened realism when their ToM practices mislead them, or when such practices point to underlying problems with self-identity.

None of this is to suggest that Iago has an adaptive or Freudian unconscious (he only technically has what Shakespeare has given us of him); as a hypothetical but mimetic construct, Iago represents intentions and motives that are hidden to himself (and others). Given our evolved, readerly propensity to track such intentions, we will naturally attach to him thoughts, emotions and motives that our available discourses would describe as sourced in different forms of conscious and unconscious mentation.[48] In doing so, we will uncover some of the limitations of cognitive theory to account for the elusive motives of a character such as Iago. Ellen Spolsky has recently called for more attention to the ordinary failures of people and their literary representations: 'The cognitive theories, for their part, in developing an account of embodiment to explain how our evolved physiology allows us to understand ourselves and to infer the beliefs, emotions, and intentions of others, is still missing examples of the ordinariness (as opposed to the brain pathology) of failure.'[49] We no doubt need to pay heed to the representation of common irrationalities or 'bounded rationality' among our fictional characters, but I argue here that cognitivists should also be mindful of what lies *between* ordinary failures and brain pathology – in this case, Iago's neurotic deceptions and self-deceptions. Such 'soft' psychological aberrations are neither as generic in nature as ordinary lapses of logic and perception, nor as 'hard' in nature as cognitive or developmental pathologies.

CHAPTER THREE

The Limits of Situated Thinking, or how Iago Gives the Lie to Cognition II

I have been arguing that, confronted with his hypermindedness or excessive theory of mind tracking, both cause and symptom of his masochistic fantasy to detach from Othello, Iago's actions lead him inexorably into a death drive and stasis. But the assumption has been that Iago's cognitive processes and strategies are purely representational (computational), walled-off from his environmental surround. Another way of saying this is that his strategizing seems to be neither embedded nor extended, and operates online with little offloading of tasks. Iago does indeed offload tasks, his cognitive strategies assisted through several instruments, most obviously Roderigo, but also Cassio and Othello himself. However, I believe that Iago's cognitive extensions worsen, rather than alleviate, his mind-reading, itself suggestive of a false dichotomy that one typically finds in cognitive and philosophical accounts of the mind between, on the one hand, internalist or representational ways of thinking (ToM) and, on the other hand, externalist, pragmatic, situated ways of thinking (extended, embedded and embodied cognition, as well as enactivism). What follows is a brief survey of recent theories of situated cognition, after which I return to Iago's inimitable way of troubling some presuppositions of cognitive theory, which will again encourage us to bring psychoanalytic theory into the picture.

It has become fashionable to talk of the 'four e's' that comprise this new situated and externalist rather than internalist view of the mind.[1] Embedded cognition, a close cousin to extended cognition, assumes that acts of cognition typically require environmental scaffolding in order to run properly. On the embedded view, cognition proper does not necessarily extend into the environment, but neural processes functionally depend on such environmental delegates.[2] Embodied cognition, more familiar to early modernists, typically assumes the mental processes are partly constituted by extra-neural bodily structures.[3] More radical anti-dualistic notions of cognitivism, much of which are influenced by phenomenology and some versions of pragmatism, are typically described as enactivist. The enacted mind acts within and on the world through the means of an intimate coupling with sensorimotor capacities and proprioception. Cognition for the enactivists amounts to a practical, skilful 'know-how', rather than knowing that something is the case.[4]

Perhaps the most provocative situated approach to cognition is the hypothesis of extended cognition. In their now famous thought experiment, Andy Clark and David Chalmers ask us to imagine two individuals, Inga and Otto, both of whom are interested in viewing an art exhibit at the Museum of Modern Art. Inga relies on her memory of the museum's location; Otto, who has Alzheimer's and is in the habit of writing information down in a notebook, consults his notebook for the location, rather than his internal memory. For Clark and Chalmers, Otto's notebook, because it serves the same functional purpose as his biological memory, extends his cognition into the environment.[5] Such cognitive extensions remind us that we are not 'brain-bound' information processors, that mental processes spill over into the world, helping us to offload tasks that would become unnecessarily burdensome if processed without external aid. Because extended cognition relies on a recursive or looping effect – cognition that is delegated to an external aid or source will modify the subject's mental states, which will in turn further alter the type of cognitive extension – Clark and Chalmers imply that the processing that takes place outside of one's head is cognitive in its own right in being functionally equivalent to internal mental states.[6] A much weaker version of extended cognition posits merely a causal nexus between brain and cognitive enhancers: Otto's notebook might indeed causally enhance his biological memory, but because it does not process information in the way that our brain does, it is not constitutive of cognition proper.[7]

All of these theories of situated cognition are deeply critical of 'in the head' cognition and the assumption that the mind is an information processor that relies on internal representations of the environment in order to function adaptively:

> It would be wrong to think that infants and animals are using some kind of theory, inferential reasoning or projective type of simulation procedure in order to make ascriptions on the basis of observed behavior ... It is much more plausible to think that cases of emotion sharing, imitation, motor mimicry and even more sophisticated contrastive emotional responses are better explained as instances of naturally calibrated reactions to the circumstances and actions of others; in normal environments we engage practically and emotionally with each other, without the need for theoretical mediation.[8]

On this radical account of situated cognition, ToM is exceedingly disembodied and mediated. Cognition seems to be a much more engaged, intersubjective, pragmatic and embodied affair than the theoretical stance would allow. Less radical critics of ToM second these objections, but note that theoretical perspective-taking still has a secondary or derivative role in cognition: 'To the extent that we do resort to a cognitive and disengaged mode of understanding one another, this practice is parasitic on the engaged, embodied, interactive dimension of our existence, and cannot therefore explain it. The order of explanation, then, is not only rejected but inverted.'[9] So, for example, while Vittorio Gallese and others have argued that empathy is signalled by the activation of mirror neurons and sensorimotor capacities, some have argued that heightened empathy is not just an intersubjective event, but requires a minimal comprehension of another's mental states, and hence ToM projections.[10] The least tendentious position is a compromise between extremes: situated and theoretical cognizing probably work in tandem, depending on local contexts and individual make-up.

To what extent can such embodied, embedded and extended theories of cognition help enhance our understanding of Iago's hypermindedness? The embodied view will not get us much further than impressing on us Iago's fantasy of disembodiment: ''Tis in ourselves, that we are thus, or thus,' Iago cautions Roderigo, 'Our bodies are gardens, to the which our wills are gardeners, so that if we will plant nettles, or sow lettuce ... supply it with one gender of herbs, or distract it with many ... why, the power, and corrigible authority of this, lies in our wills' (1.3.319–26). Iago claims that we can reorient bodily desires at will, that pure exercises of rationality can cool the 'raging motions' and 'carnal stings' that his bestiary-minded tropes ascribe to animals. And Iago at least convinces Othello that his words and thoughts regarding Desdemona's infidelity are dispassionate truths, 'close denotements, working from the heart, / That passion cannot rule' (3.3.127–8). Othello's comment here belies any neat dualism that Iago puts into practice, for if Iago's notions come from the 'heart', they are still at least metaphorically embodied. The important point is not whether Iago can make good on his advocacy of disem-bodiment, but that it seems to be a fantasy that he holds dear, and that he can put to instrumental effect.

Iago's seeming negative empathy can help us test the relevance of the embedded–enactive view to his character.

Evan Thompson positions this neurophenomenological view of empathy against both ToM and simulation theories: 'In empathy we experience another human being directly as a person – that is, as an intentional being whose bodily gestures and actions are expressive of his or her experiences of states of mind.'[11] Thompson's enactive typology of empathy posits a passive or involuntary sensorimotor coupling at a purely affective level (which is consistent with recent findings in mirror neuron research), in which we experience another as a living body by 'experiencing or sharing each other's unconscious body schemas'.[12] In addition to affective coupling, one also finds in empathy a transposition of oneself into the place of the other, but such perspective-taking is not purely cognitive, and does not assume that the first-person perspective 'comes first and serves as a basis for developing understanding of the other'.[13] Not only do first- and third-person understandings 'develop together out of a prior experience of intentional relations', but 'reiterated empathy' suggests that the very basis of seeing oneself as an 'individual participant in an intersubjective world' assumes that one must see oneself from the perspective of the other.

On the neurophenomenological or enactivist account, empathy is thus the lived, bodily experience of another that privileges a second-person, intersubjective encounter. I think that anyone who has imagined what it is like to be Iago can see that his manner of empathizing is at best a radically first-person version of cognitive empathy, an example of the solipsistic view of empathy that the neurophenomenological account would reject. How does Iago know what he knows about Othello? 'These Moors are changeable in their wills,' (1.3.347) he assures Roderigo, a hypothesis which, not incidentally, follows immediately from Iago's own assertion that he is master of his own will: ''Tis in ourselves that we are thus, or thus' (1.3.319–20). This sort of cognitive empathy, in which Iago *knows* what Othello will do and feel, rather than *feels* what Othello will do and feel, is derived from a contrast between his sense of himself as Stoically impassive and

Othello as a type of person who is constitutionally capricious. I have already described Iago as a theory of mind zombie: this is a character whose very phenomenological distance from embedded, bodily, reiterative intersubjectivity allows him the ability to construct images of Othello, Cassio and Desdemona that serve him well practically, if not psychically. As with the embodied approach, the enactive approach is useful in its heuristic value if only because Iago's aversion to such forms of situated cognition function as reaction-formations and symptoms of more complex psychic mechanisms at work.

The most useful heuristic that we can borrow from situated cognition, however, is the extended mind hypothesis. I would emphasize at the outset that in no purely cognitive sense does Iago extend his thinking into the environment. It would be misleading to suggest that his instrumental reliance on an easy mark such as Roderigo or Cassio, or his manipulation of Othello's trust in order to advance his plans, are examples of extended cognition proper. If we take the mark of the cognitive to include information processing, deductive reasoning, memory enhancement and the like, then Roderigo, for example, someone who hardly enhances Iago's calculations, clearly does not serve as Iago's cognitive delegate.[14] Furthermore, given the paramount secrecy of Iago's scheming, one naturally expects that his circumstances militate against such cognitive extension. Yet we should not dismiss the implications of extended cognition entirely, for what does seem relevant to the advancement of Iago's project is a basic presupposition of extended cognition, namely, that we think and act more efficiently when we offload tasks to external vehicles. It is precisely the interplay between what Iago offloads and what he on-loads that can help us understand the unexpected consequences of his instrumental use of his several dupes.

Enlisting Roderigo to be conjunctive with him against Othello (for the right 'purse'), Iago philosophizes on the virtues of wilful autonomy as an antidote to Roderigo's despair over his unrequited love for Desdemona. As we have already seen, Iago's argument is for radical disembodiment born of his manipulation of the dualistic presuppositions of faculty psychology: reason controls will, and will controls those carnal and bodily appetites that separate our humanity from the sensibility of a 'baboon' (1.3.316). That the virtue of perdurable self-reliance and wilful autonomy is a mere fantasy that Iago holds about himself is conveyed in the embodied language he uses later, for example, in his admission that the very thought of Othello's having leapt into his seat 'gnaw[s]' his 'inwards' (2.1.292), pointing to a visceral response unmistakably lodged in his body. But we have also seen that Iago's fantasy holds sway over others: Othello will later take note of Iago's hidden thoughts 'working from the heart, / That passion cannot rule' (3.3.127–8), implying that he too believes that Iago thinks and acts dispassionately.

We shouldn't conflate Iago's praise of the autonomy of will with an argument for self-reliance, since he realizes even before his plan has taken shape that he will need to rely on Roderigo as an instrument in deceiving Othello. Although Iago promises that, through an exercise of his 'wits' (1.3.358), Roderigo will 'enjoy' Desdemona, part of such an exercise depends on Roderigo's complicity, the results of which will supposedly redound to both: 'If thou canst cuckold him, thou doest thyself a pleasure, and me a sport. There are many events in the womb of time, which will be delivered' (1.3.368–70). After a tacit commitment from Roderigo, Iago opens his first soliloquy with a puzzling defensive gesture:

> Thus do I ever make my fool my purse:
> For I mine own gain'd knowledge should profane,
> If I would time expend with such a snipe,
> But for my sport and profit.

> (1.3.381–3)

Iago's reference to 'gained knowledge' is curious. Knowledge of the ways in which bodily attempts can suborn the will without the vigilance of reason? Knowledge of the way in which Moors generally are 'changeable in their wills' or women generally 'must change for youth'? Both forms of knowledge are generalizable, even theoretical, based on inference, but Iago claims that he has 'gained' such knowledge, as if it is conditioned by experience. Iago's inferences carry such evidentiary force that he draws no distinction between inferential and empirical or situated knowledge. But he seems to apologize for divulging such knowledge to the low-born Roderigo, as if to share that knowledge would be to expend or, given the economic language of the exchange, spend that knowledge unwisely, even contaminate such knowledge by 'profanation'.

The important point is that the process of offloading information to an instrument such as Roderigo enhances rather than appeases Iago's sense of vulnerability. However anxious his (on-loaded) hypermindedness renders him, Iago's distribution of his scheming (as well as some of his constitutional bile) to an auditor like Roderigo compounds, rather than eases, any cognitive and emotional burdens that he bears. The transition from his first extended exchange with Roderigo to the subsequent monologue shows that extending his mind paradoxically has the effect of bringing Iago back to himself with a vengeance. Consider the important non sequitur near the beginning of his first monologue, just after Roderigo has exited. After assuring himself that time spent with Roderigo will not profane his knowledge, since it is for sport and profit, Iago declares, 'I hate the Moor, / And it is thought abroad, that 'twixt my sheets / He's done my office' (1.3.385–6). The very process of airing his views to another renders him more introspective, which feeds his overthinking (in this case regarding Othello's imagined actions against him), in turn furthering his alienation. The psychological perils of such offloading occur in the next exchange between Roderigo and Iago, this time when Iago works to convince Roderigo that Desdemona's 'very nature' will compel her to consummate with Cassio. The conversation helps to convince Roderigo to supplant Cassio, prompting Iago's further ruminations on Othello's having cuckolded him and his exclamation that he will never be 'content' until he is 'even' with the Moor (2.1.293–4).

How can we understand this vicious circle? On one simple level, Iago's conversation with and enlisting of Roderigo has the effect of further developing his plot, which then requires that he think afresh about his next moves, registered in his 'Let me see now' (1.3.390) and his decision to 'abuse Othello's ear' (1.3.393) with the notion that Cassio is too familiar with Desdemona. The preceding expressions about his hatred of the Moor for his suspected cuckolding of him are the means by which Iago works himself up to his scheming, perhaps quietly justifying it. But the danger here is to assume that the uneasiness bred of Iago's hatred of Othello is just a rationalized excuse for the scheme that will provide him sadistic pleasure. Rather, the scheme itself is orchestrated to relieve the discontentment that his obsessive thinking has been causing.

Iago does extend his mind, then, with the caveat that such extensions carry an indissoluble mix of strategic, emotional and cognitive information: strategic because Roderigo becomes constitutive to his developing scheme; emotional because he incites in Roderigo the same hatred that he carries for Othello (which then bolsters that hatred of Othello); and philosophical because his theories and inferences about human behaviour are ratified by Roderigo's service – Iago's belief that Roderigo is a fool in his purse is confirmed by Roderigo's too-easy compliance, and his belief in the power of the will is verified by his own easy exercise of authority over Roderigo. But if Iago transfers some mental content, the net result of these extensions is to remind himself not only of his hatred of Othello, but of the very admission that his hatred is based simply on his perception that Othello is abusing him. To communicate his views on Othello and Desdemona, and to coax Roderigo into believing that he and Roderigo can undermine Othello, function as *cognitively contagious* for Iago in that this further confirms, through his own surmises, that he is the prototypical cuckold. Consider the relevance here of the notion of looping cognition, an important feature of the extended mind hypothesis: 'As with a turbo-driven engine that uses the very exhaust it produces to increase its own power, a cognitive system will on occasion structure the environment in a manner that enhances its abilities, which in turn enables it to structure the environment more effectively, enhancing its abilities further, and so on.'[15] Here we have a cognitivist explanation for what is described in more folk-psychological terms as Iago's improvisational ability. But again, although Iago's improvisations do enable him to refine his plot and enhance his strategic 'abilities', they have the psychological effect of furthering his disgruntlement.

When we argue that Iago supplements his interior scheming with situated cognition, we immediately confront the limitations of any application of situated cognition to the irreducible mentalizing of a character such as Iago. His counterintuitive thinking can have real-life parallels that are often overlooked by a philosophical and cognitive approach that extrapolates theories of mind and body from ideally rational agents. This is a criticism that has been made against the parity principle of extended and embodied cognition, in particular:

We often want to understand the specificities of particular embodied subjects: just why and how one system – such as a particular embodied agent of one kind or another – can move between a variety of different artifacts... Mainstream psychology has long studied individual differences in the way people approach various cognitive tasks without significant use of external resources. So, likewise, even in tasks which can involve extended looping and coupling cognition, we're all familiar with folk who *aren't* content or able to leave the information out there in the world ... It would be silly, for most purposes, to try to *keep track of* what shelf everything in the refrigerator is currently on; if and when you want something, just *look* ... But we all know people who do typically upload such information into their onboard biological memories: such individual differences in the amount and style of reliance on external resources are often glaring in the way people plan and engage in complex activities.[16]

The question, then, is not simply *whether* or *how* one goes about offloading tasks in order to lighten one's mental load, but *why* some individuals might seem irrationally to choose not to offload or, as with Iago, why such offloading might paradoxically carry burdensome weight but be carried out nonetheless. And as our application of ToM to Iago led into a psychoanalytic approach, so too our application of situated thinking calls out for an explanatory supplement, psychoanalytic theory providing one such alternative model. What would a psychoanalytic interpretation of the vicious on-loading/offloading cycle look like? Iago's peculiar habit of ruminating on perceived offenses just after he has expressed his views (both philosophical and pragmatic) to Roderigo, an example of looping cognition in cognitivist terms, can be seen as example of *countertransference* in psychoanalytic terms. Unlike transference, in which the analysand projects otherwise unconscious desires and beliefs on to the analyst (the analyst reflects those principal figures in the analysand's life who are motivating the analysand's pathology or trauma), countertransference assumes that the analyst in turn projects unconscious wishes or beliefs on to the patient. Whether lecturing Roderigo and Othello on faculty psychology and the importance of free will, Stoic apathy, the virtues of patience or the canons of manliness, Iago clearly casts himself as therapist and pedagogue. But what typically happens is that his therapeutic advice agitates his own suppressed views regarding comparable matters, and he responds with further hostility toward perceived insults. Despite the discontentment such musings bring, his perverse (anti)-therapeutic advice to others ironically is introjected such that he becomes that very anti-therapist to himself.

The ideational content of countertransference is typically linked to primary processes or unconscious thoughts and impulses. Recall that the emergence into consciousness of

Iago's excessive ToM tracking serves as a symptom, one that keeps him detached from others, allowing him to disavow through a reaction-formation his biographical and ontological nullity (in Lacanian terms the symptom keeps him from directly encountering the pre-subjective Real, even as it announces the Real's underlying presence). To deny, negate or overcome the symptom would be to re-engage the Real, which would conduce to a symbolic death. To extend, situate, or instrumentalize his plans and cognitions obviously works to further Iago's plot, the very *telos* of which is not simply the destruction of Othello, but Iago's bringing down of himself, in all probability leading to his literal death. In terms simply of the trajectory of Iago's development in the play, offloading tends to contribute to Iago's eventual demise, despite its local successes in achieving his cuckolding plot. From early on, Roderigo shows his recalcitrance, complaining that he has not been remunerated for his money (2.3.355); nor does his willingness to murder Cassio appease his own frustration with Iago. Iago realizes as much but soldiers on with his plan:

> I have rubb'd this young quat almost to the sense,
> And he grows angry now ... Live Roderigo,
> He calls me to a restitution large,
> For gold and jewels, that I bobb'd from him,
> As gifts to Desdemona.

> (5.1.11–17)

To rub Roderigo this way (which might have been avoided, since the imaginative Iago could have carried out his plan without fleecing Roderigo in the process) has dire consequences regarding the eventual sentencing of Iago: the decisive incriminating of Iago and Lodovico's testimony of Iago's 'cunning cruelty' (5.2.334) are warranted by Roderigo's letter testifying that Iago 'set him on' (5.2.330). Another way of saying this is that, as Robert Heilman points out, Iago is a dangerously compulsive gambler, one whose resentful malice runs so perversely wild that 'it contains something of the suicidal'.[17]

En route to that literal death, however, Iago achieves, through masochism, the fantasy of separating from Othello by forcing Othello to impose paternal law and hire Iago as his mock officer in the plot to bring down Cassio (and eventually, Desdemona). The cycle is such that each time Iago offloads and advances his plot, his ToM discontentment increases, which requires more plotting and extending, the consequence of which is the production of incriminating evidence against him. Situatedness serves as handmaiden to the death drive, contributing really to Iago's 'two deaths': the eventual negation of his obsessive belief-attributions and the literal torturing and presumed death that await him.

There is still another way in which situated cognition might be explained in the context of psychoanalytic models of repression. Consider that fetish objects, which enable disavowal by standing in for traumatic events or recognition, integrate the subject's psyche with the world of external objects. Since, prior to therapy, disavowal is not ordinarily a conscious strategy, fetish objects tend to maintain or regulate unconscious beliefs and desires: fetish objects *link* the external world with the psychoanalytic unconscious. Might we not say that the analogue to the cognitivist situated or extended mind is, in psychoanalytic discourse, the *extended unconscious*? Recall that one of Iago's impasses is that, prior to his scheming, he has failed repeatedly to acquire the handkerchief that might have served as an appropriate fetish object to allow for his separation from Othello. We might interpret all other forms of Iago's conscious situatedness or externalism (whether cognitive or otherwise), as compensations for his inability to extend himself through the means of fetishistic disavowal. If this is true, why does the eventual acquisition of the handkerchief not give Iago the needed defensive symbol? At the point that he has acquired the handkerchief, his stratagems are well under way, his sado-masochism providing him not simply with an alternative form of disavowal, but one that, because it is directly linked to his death drive, allows for a retreat further from the comforts of the pleasure principle: the handkerchief acquires an instrumental, abjective status over both its objective and symbolic status. What had initially served as a potential object of disavowal is itself negated in the service of what I will be describing in the next chapter as Iago's sublimely tragic pursuit of death and evasion of his own neural sublime.

CHAPTER FOUR

Tragic Catharsis: Escaping the Neural Sublime

Because Iago exits quietly, seemingly without a trace of *anagnorisis*, Iago's best critics have refused him (and implicitly the playgoer) the expulsion of pity and fear. Following Kenneth Burke's remark that the best Iago gives us is oxymoronic 'filthy purgation', Edward Pechter remarks: '"What you know, you know" does more than just [alert] us ... to the failure of Iago's exertions to lead to any nourishing insight. Its circularity acts out the futility of our own exertions – a reverse *anagnorisis* for us too. Nothing is revealed, no curative reorganization achieved ... Whatever catharsis meant for Aristotle and whatever it means for us, it is not here ... What we get from Iago, or rather what we get from our own desires for an Iagocentric *Othello*, is an unexpiated and perhaps unexpiatable guilt.'[1] Pechter's view is echoed in Richard Raatzsch's gloss on Iago's epistemological tautology, 'What you know, you know' (5.2.304): 'He does not defend himself; he does not repent; he does not pray; he does not show any reaction to the threat of torture ... He certainly does not undergo any moral awakening or purification, which would allow him to accept and be reconciled to his fate.'[2] For Raatzsch, Iago's character is neatly summarized as 'destruction without catharsis'.[3] But we move too quickly when we deny

Iago such purgation. Moral awakenings are the marrow of Christian tragedy, not this particular Shakespearean tragedy; and purification is one of the most vexed ideas associated with tragic definitions, from Aristotle onward.

Aristotle's discussion of the effects of tragedy in the *Nicomachean Ethics* and *Rhetoric* is sufficiently ambiguous as to warrant three competing interpretations of catharsis: the purifying, purgative and educative accounts of the transformation of pity and fear. The purification thesis, which holds that pain cultivated through identification is eventually transformed into pleasure, has become the least convincing these days, since it assumes that, insofar as the emotions of pity and fear need to be purified, there is something intrinsically impure or befouled about such identificatory emotional responses.[4] The purgative view has to recommend it the etymological root of catharsis, namely, menstruation, suggesting by analogy an emotional discharge. In the *Politics*, Aristotle specifically describes catharsis as a cure for the pathological condition of religious frenzy: 'Some persons fall into a religious frenzy, whom we see as a result of the sacred melodies – when they have used the melodies that excite the soul to mystic frenzy – restored as though they had found healing and catharsis.'[5] This goes a way toward justifying the notion that catharsis is akin to a medical purge.[6] The educative or pedagogical viewpoint, fashionable among recent scholars of Aristotle, assumes that, because Aristotle held a cognitive view of the emotions (emotions are not raw feelings, but rather beliefs that provide an orientation to the world), tragic drama helps the apprentice in virtue to reorient his emotional set: 'Tragedy provides (a mimesis of) certain objects toward which it is appropriate to form certain beliefs and evaluative attitudes as well as to feel certain pains.'[7]

Iago meets conditions for *both* the purgative and purificatory accounts of cathartic resolution, even putting the latter in service of the former. 'And calm of mind all passion spent' is the echoing choral paean to Samson Agonistes in Milton's Aristotelian tragedy. Does not the becalmed Iago anticipate at least the spent but purged Samson? Purged of what, in Iago's case? Precisely the cognitive noise that I have been at pains to elaborate, which requires us to appreciate that Aristotle's view of the emotions is neither biologically reductionistic nor Galenic; and that at least one physiological site of purgation in Shakespeare's play is Iago's cognitive make-up. A. D. Nuttall reminds us that Aristotle argues analogically when describing catharsis as a medical purge: 'As the body seeks to ease its load of waste matter, so the soul – the higher faculty if you like terms of value – seeks to ease its burden of emotion.'[8] If we add some Freud to Aristotle, we find that Iago's very masochistic efforts provide the means by which he can purge himself of his hypermindedness (his 'psychic discharges'). If his scheming, masochistic efforts (a first-order catharsis) help him to transform his ToM pains into pleasure (a purification of *too much* cognition through the route of the desiderata of inverted sadism), his quiescent vanishing from the play marks the moment at which he has purged or expelled his cognitive symptomatology (a second-order catharsis).

But what of our tragic identification with Iago and ensuing catharsis? In terms of tragic identification, we quite easily, if surprisingly, relate to Iago's *manner of thinking*, if not to the excesses to which he puts such thinking. As I have noted, Aristotle was something of a cognitivist in his own right: since emotions are always linked to evaluative judgements and beliefs (anger, for example, will always take an intentional object), identification with tragic figures rests on a shared intellectual or cognitive attunement, not merely empathy issuing from free-floating emotions. The ToM assumption that we ferret out the hidden intentions and beliefs is precisely what makes identification with Iago ready at hand. Although theories of situated cognition have downgraded the centrality of 'in the head' cognition, we are like Iago perhaps more than we are like any other Shakespearean principal, if only to the extent that his over-riding trait of mind-reading is one of our basic cognitive abilities. Hence the pleasure we get from reading Iago's mind is not fundamentally different from the pleasure Iago gets from reading the minds of his peers.

Perhaps it is true that tragic catharsis is not as easily achievable for Iago as it is for us. But rather than assume that the web of identification disintegrates at the point at which Iago's scheming becomes too far removed from us for its diabolism, which will be something of a rationalization for many (some have even argued that, as a professional schemer, Iago's actions are admirable), I suggest that our identification slackens at the moment when Iago achieves the calmness that marks his own catharsis.[9] And it slackens because, as zealous critics and over-readers of Iago's motives, we obsess over his intentions just as he obsesses over the intentions and beliefs of his peers. Consider that my very thesis – that masochism allows Iago to negate his hyperattunement to others, thereby affording him release – uses psychoanalytic theory to create the conditions of catharsis that I am forced to deny myself; i.e. my claim that psychoanalysis helps explain Iago's escape from overthinking relies on my relentless thinking about his hidden intentions. To puzzle over Iago's motives (I am not alone in this, of course) is not to pathologize ourselves but to deny ourselves the very purgation of obsessive mind-reading that we, as cognitivists and psychoanalytic critics, project on to Iago. Put in terms of the educative theory of tragedy: the arc of Iago's astonishingly changeful character – from immeasurable quanta of psychic energy to cognitive stasis – provides a cognitive, if not moralistic exemplum about the potential perils of mind-reading.

Iago between the ancients and moderns

What of Iago's place in the context of the *history* of tragedy? Is he more akin to an ancient or modern hero (or anti-hero)? Does he defy such tidy categorizations? Influenced by Hegel's substantive view of ancient tragedy, Kierkegaard asserts that characters in Greek tragedy are subordinated to overarching ideological determinants, while characters in modern tragedies exert unqualified free will and heightened subjectivity: 'In ancient tragedy, the action itself has an epic element; it is just as much event as action. This, of course, is because the ancient world did not have subjectivity reflected in itself ... Modern tragedy has no epic foreground, no epic remainder. The hero stands and falls entirely on his own deeds.'[10] For Kierkegaard, however, an authentic modern tragedy could only emerge when the bad faith of the modern sensibility would be offset by a reintroduction of some overarching structure (whether secular or sacred) that contextualizes the hero's actions and provides for limited conflict (although such conflict need not be neatly resolved according to the Hegelian strictures of sublation): 'A truly modern tragedy would incorporate modernity's heightened reflection into the "substantial" world of antiquity, but would not eliminate aesthetic ambiguity by resolving the conflict for the sake of ethical clarity.'[11]

Despite the hand-wringing over what distinguishes moral from amoral actions of characters in any tragedy, the difference between ancient and modern tragedy amounts to what sociologists such as Pierre Bourdieu or Anthony Giddens would describe as a fundamental tension between structure and agency (the ethos of Kierkegaard's 'truly modern' tragic hero comports with Bourdieu's *habitus* in its mediation of will and determinism).[12] But how to think of the relationship between cognitivism/evolutionary psychology, on the one hand, and tragic character, action and emplotment, on the other? Once we determine the neurological correlates responsible for basic human (and non-human) striving, have we not invigorated structure over agency? We are told again and again by cognitive theorists that so much of adaptive cognition is subpersonal and that, for those who extend such neuro-reductionism to consciousness itself, we are indeed 'strangers to ourselves' or 'egoless' selves.[13] Consider then the ToM that motors Iago's scheming is akin to a structured biological inheritance that serves as an analogue to Hegel's 'substantive ... powers that influence the human will: family love between husband and wife ... political life ... the will of the ruler ...'[14] If we, too, the mindful readers of Iago's intentionality, are directed by some of the subpersonal processes that seem to govern him, we marvel not simply at his likeness to us, but at his tendency toward working through (exercising exquisite, if covert agency) some of the potentially handicapping elements of those modes of subpersonalism that, under certain circumstances, can begin to seep into conscious thinking . I emphasize *tendency* to work through, because if there is catharsis for us, it occurs when we realize and reject the extent of the malevolent measures that Iago will pursue in order to find the peace of mind that has eluded him from the outset. At that point the human costs of contentment far outweigh the means, and our (cognitive) empathy with him is expelled. But perhaps what makes Iago a contemporary, rather than ancient or modern, tragic figure is that his example can at least help us to see, as I have described earlier, not only the superficialities of the rational therapies of cognitive-behaviourism in its neo-Stoic incarnations, but also the limitations of the scientific–medical approach of diagnostic psychiatry, the latter of which, having little tolerance for depth psychology and dynamic psychology, would isolate and treat symptomatology, but with little regard to motive.[15]

Death drive redux

Astonished by the fact that the dreams of traumatic neurosis repeatedly bring patients to the original accident or trauma, Freud conceptually located the death drive 'beyond' the pleasure principle. Under its normal functioning, the mind is oriented toward discharging or diffusing unwanted energy, the pleasure principle serving to decrease tension. Traumatic neuroses present the mind with pathological stimuli that escape mitigation by the pleasure principle and seem to serve needs that are more primitive than gaining or avoiding pleasure.[16] The disruptions that mark such compulsions to repeat suggested to Freud the primordial drive toward death and stasis, a remarkable idea that compelled Freud to import an entirely new teleological principle into the history of psychoanalysis.[17]

But what if, as Jonathan Lear asks, the self-disruptions that Freud attached to a compulsion to repeat and drive toward death are *not for anything at all* – 'devoid of purpose', and so disruptive of teleology as such?[18] What if, like Darwin's random mutations and self-disruptions of nature (which carry only *as if* teleology), a psychic disruption or traumatic repetition is an 'aborted attempt at mindedness – not, as Freud thinks, a directed movement of the mind'?[19] The death drive would become, in Lear's terms, a seduction, the enigmatic signifier that Freud requires in order to maintain his overarching view that the mind is teleological and goal-directed. But to understand Lear's revisionism, one must extrapolate from mental self-disruptions a radical conception of normal, non-pathological life as always potentially overwhelming, such normal life experienced as constitutionally fragile and under the threat of trauma:

> From a psychoanalytic point of view, there are two distinct senses in which *life is too much*. First, there is the structural insight that life is lived under conditions of tension. For the mind to discharge all tension, to achieve a completely unpressured state, is precisely what it is for it to die. This was Freud's structural insight in *Beyond the Pleasure Principle*. In this sense, it is basically a structural truth that life is too much. Second, because we are always and everywhere living under pressure, we must live with the possibility of a breakthrough in any psychological structure we have thus far achieved. In part, this is due to the fact that psychological structure is itself a psychological achievement. It is a response to previous experiences of loss and gain – and as such is constitutionally vulnerable.[20]

The significance of self-disruptions, normal occurrences given the 'too muchness' of life, is completely open-ended; such disruptions are neither intrinsically good nor bad but, as Lear points out, exist 'before good and evil'. Whether they attach themselves to healthy or unhealthy desires or actions depends upon 'what happens next', that is, depends upon the 'entire previous history of happenings next'.[21]

An Aristotelian philosopher also trained as a psycho-analyst, Lear is neither a cognitive theorist nor literary critic. But his insights have profound implications for the assumptions and methods of literary cognitivism that I have been so far tracking. What is Iago's excessive intentionality, his cognition gone awry, if not an example of (or analogue to) the psychoanalytic notion of psychic excess, quanta of energy, or 'too much' that Lear invokes? But the difference between us and Iago (between the literary embodiment of mind-reading and the lived experience thereof) is that Iago _motivates his own self-disruptions_ through the very practice of disrupting Othello's equanimity. And those disruptions (the full complement of his sadomasochism and its consequences) drive him toward not simply death but the very teleological principle that, if Lear is correct, is really a sham principle for us: a seductive remainder or enigmatic signifier that makes sense of the interpretive overload of which ToM, in its extreme manifestations, is a symptom. It is precisely Iago's putting into place what I describe below as his escape from the neural sublime that provides him with such an elusive form of catharsis.

Escaping the neural sublime

In his _Critique of Judgement_, Kant remarks that the dynamical sublime 'is to be found in a formless object, insofar as in it or by occasion of it boundlessness is represented, and yet its totality is also present to thought'.[22] The sublime object or event exceeds the capacity of our sense or imagination, but simultaneously elevates the supersensible power of reason to at least intuit something transcendent and absolutely great. While there have been several important pre- and post-Kantian variations of the sublime, most such versions see the sublime as fostering a suspension of the ego in the face of some ruptural event or object that brings the subject into contact with a numinous unitary being. The 'neural sublime' is the most recent variation on our thinking of the sublime. Drawing on Edmund Burke's material concept of the sublime – if for Kant the sublime idealizes reason, and 'erases the body', for Burke, the sublime is fundamentally a corporeal experience – Alan Richardson contends that the 'neural sublime yields up a disturbing but compulsive glimpse into the ordinarily secret workings of the brain'.[23] What Richardson means by such 'secret workings of the brain' is typically the cognitive unconscious: as neuroscientists are fond of pointing out, the reality that the brain constructs for us (which the mind perceives) is often a partial, illusory, or 'low-salience' version of the external world. The fact that we do not ordinarily perceive the material blind spots in our visual field, or that a Necker cube seems to flip entirely at random – or that, as 'motion blindness' has revealed, we are often ignorant of background figures when observing foreground motion – suggests that the world as consciously perceived is often a series of simulacra: that it is epistemologically inaccessible. To catch a glimpse of the material substrate of the brain at work, below the level of mental awareness/perception, constitutes for Richardson a sublime moment: 'Perhaps the sublime moment constitutes "a genuine experience of what is, or seems to be, inaccessible to ordinary and familiar modes of epistemological access".'[24] To compare (very) large things to (very) small ones, this would make the sublime experience analogous to perceiving the blind spot in our visual field.'[25] The truly sublime experience would be one in which we are brought to the 'shock' of realizing simultaneously that our habitual perceptions are illusory – an 'intuition of nothingness' – and that we cannot genuinely access the material substrate conjuring such illusoriness. The sublime moment is lodged between the breakdown of ordinary consciousness and intuitive positing of the cognitive unconscious, or the brain as such.

According to Richardson, Keats meditates in *Endymion* on those forms of cognizing that 'dodge / Conception to the very bourne of heaven, / Then leave the naked brain', an example of the poet's tendency to evince the neural sublime by imaginatively deriving a brain void of perceptual consciousness, itself paradoxically a symbol of the mind's power: 'This very experience of conscious quietude and conceptual emptiness provides a glimpse into the underlying presence and workings of the brain in all its nakedness. The brain's voidness in such moments paradoxically comes to signify the mind's power as its ultimate limits.'[26] Shelley, too, invokes the naked/sublime brain in his description, in the 'Triumph of Life', of the momentary wiping away of his consciousness – 'And suddenly my brain became as sand' – about which Richardson remarks: 'In place of the idealist notion of thought without a brain, here is a brain bereft of thought – the mind's instantiation in brain revealed by its momentary extinction.'[27] Regarding these passages and several others, Richardson bracingly concludes that the Romantic neural sublime, unlike the Kantian sublime, is fundamentally a material sublime, a 'brain's-eye view of the world' in which we can access not the idealized, transcendent supersensible, but the subsensible realm, the physiological neural mechanisms working beneath our perceptual illusions. Analogous to the ecological sublime – described by Christopher Hitt as Thoreau's novel manner of achieving transcendence with nature itself – the neural sublime exalts the brain itself, 'which grows strange, awesome, and of titanic proportions in relation to the conscious subject, overwhelming it and yet leaving it with a sense of what Wordsworth calls "possible sublimity".'[28]

Why assume, though, that such a glimpse of our material, operational brain, the cognitive nonconscious beneath perceptual consciousness, would provide the paradoxical terror/pleasure that constitutes such a 'neural sublime?' I have been arguing all along that it is the very coming to consciousness of such an ordinarily nonconscious brain process as ToM attunement that, in Iago's case, fuels his discontentment and death drive. The upsurging of this 'neural sublime', this 'brain's-eye' view of the world (which might more accurately be described as a *neuroreductive sublime*) is precisely what Iago is at pains to negate. Not an empty, voided or naked brain, not a brain devoid of consciousness, but consciousness devoid of brain – that is Iago's fantasy, a fantasy that would give the lie to neuroreductionism as well as phenomenology in its desire to imagine consciousness without *intentionality*, an impossibly pure and undirected perception that is unattached to the external world.

In his tendency to negate, in pursuit of masochism and death, this intentionality that has become too much a part of his conscious will, Iago's sublimely tragic figuration can best be understood in the context of those philosophers like Schopenhauer who link the sublime to an embrace of the death principle.[29] Here is Schopenhauer on the tragic sublime:

> Our pleasure in the tragedy belongs not to the feeling of the beautiful, but to that of the sublime ... For, just as at the sight of the sublime in nature we turn away from the interest of the will, so in the tragic catastrophe we turn away from the will-to-live itself. Thus in the tragedy the terrible side of life is presented to us ... and so that aspect of the world is brought before our eyes which directly opposes our will away from life, to give up willing and loving life. But precisely in this way we become aware that there is still left in us something different that we cannot possibly know positively, but only negatively, as that which does not will life ... At the moment of the tragic catastrophe, we become convinced more clearly than ever that life is a bad dream from which we have to awake ... The effect of the tragedy is analogous to that of the dynamically sublime, since, like this, it raises us above the will and its interest, and puts us

in such a mood that we find pleasure in the sight of what directly opposes the will ... In this the tragic spirit consists; accordingly it leads to resignation.[30]

The *interests of Iago's will*, the sum total of his schemes and intentions against others, are what he displaces in the play, in spite of (or because of) his assurance to Roderigo: "Tis in ourselves, that we are thus, or thus: our bodies are our gardens, to the which our wills are gardeners' (1.3.319–21). What happens when our ordinary, cognizable will becomes too much our 'corrigible authority' (1.3.326) such that we are not 'thus or thus' but just creatures of our encompassing desires to imagine the intentions and beliefs of others? Iago uncannily confronts his own 'neural sublime', his tragedy being that he puts that very exceptional intentionality to his own destruction. 'Demand me nothing, what you know, you know' (5.2.304). Here is that rare form of tragic 'resignation' that Schopenhauer could not find in the Greeks: Oedipus at Colonus shows resignation, but finds comfort in the prospect of revenge on his native land; Cassandra too finds solace in revenge; Hercules dies composed but not resigned. The moderns, however, are at a much 'higher level' than the ancients ('Shakespeare is much greater than Sophocles').[31] The tragic in Iago, in keeping with Schopenhauer's worldview, lies in his ability to 'turn away the will from life', tragedy's 'true tendency', and to embrace death resignedly, contentedly.

Iago has been frequently called a solipsist. What gets left out of such appraisals is the sublimely tragic quality of that solipsism. Through an encounter with the sublime 'we feel ourselves reduced to nothing; we feel ourselves as individuals, as living bodies, as transient phenomena of will, like drops in the ocean, dwindling and dissolving into nothing. But against such a ghost of our own nothingness ... there arises the immediate consciousness that all these worlds exist only in our representation, only as modifications of the pure subject of knowing'.[32] If for Burke and Kant, as well as the theorists of the neural sublime, the sublime encounter is expansive, putting us in touch with wider natural, material and neuro-logical absolutes, for Schopenhauer, the sublime encounter is contractive, putting us in touch with an absolute ego for which the entire world exists only as that ego's representation: 'The vastness of the world, which previously disturbed our peace of mind, now rests within us; our dependence on it is now annulled by its dependence on us.'[33] The vastness of Iago's representational world – his very unsettling dependence on the full gamut of his representational and situated cognition – is subject not to expansion but to contraction and annulment at the moment of his resigned confrontation with his own demise. While we would go too far to say that Iago has become a 'pure subject of knowing', we can say that his metaphysical solipsism works to displace the neural sublime, which would include both his own representational/computational thinking and his situated or embedded cognition. His solipsism works not to dismantle but to reify or suspend the problem of other minds, what we might describe as a *neuroreactionary* impetus behind his world-withdrawal.

The philosopher Daniel Dennett, who has asserted that consciousness is nothing more than a 'physical, biological phenomenon', expresses dismay that he is too often forced into the role of spoilsport, compelled to assure his audiences that consciousness is 'the most wonderful magic show imagi-nable'.[34] But perhaps Iago is the consummate magician not because of, but in spite of, his aptitude for belief-attribution. Iago's example suggests to us that, beyond such cognitive skills, and beyond all symbolic investitures, there is some leftover quiddity of consciousness that is more than mere smoke and mirrors. And I believe that we approach, but can only circle around, those aspects of Iago that seem irreducible to his cognitive mastery precisely when we hunt for his motives. If Iago were a cyborg or zombie who thinks exactly like us, but who lacks perceptual consciousness or a 'what it is like' to be that cyborg or zombie, we would look for a *reason*, not a *motive* for that being's seemingly inexplicable turn toward evil. We would say that the cyborg malfunctioned, or that the zombie's thoughts just turned toward malevolence. But to project a motive implies *something else* beyond that creature's (or character's) baseline cognizing that impels its action, a perceptual awareness or consciousness that announces its numinous presence even as it eludes our efforts at reductivism. And I would go so far as to say that, despite Iago's refusal to testify to anything at the end of the play, he seems more, not less 'conscious' than before – we cannot put a content to that consciousness, and it can only be experienced by us as something that seems to have survived the hollowing out of the cognitive contents of his mind, but despite the voidness of his brain at the end of the play, there seems to be something that it is like to be Iago, after all.

CHAPTER FIVE

From Mindblindness to Extended Mind: The Othello Problem

To what extent is Othello, in terms of the mind-reading–mindblindness continuum, a foil to Iago? If Iago's offloading of his scheme to Roderigo and Othello paradoxically renders him more discontented, what can we conclude about Othello's offloading and extension of his cognitions to Iago? Unable to discern, for example, what Iago 'think[s]' about Cassio (3.3.108), Othello exclaims in frustration:

> Think, my lord? By heaven, he echoes me,
> As if there were some monster in his thought,
> Too hideous to be shown ...
> As if thou then hadst shut up in thy brain
> Some horrible conceit: If thou dost love me,
> Show me thy thought.
>
> (3.3.110–12, 117–20)

The success of Iago's inveigling depends on his convincing Othello that he knows more than he lets on: 'This honest creature doubtless / Sees and knows more, much more, than he unfolds' (3.3.246–7). Iago does not simply exploit Othello's credulousness; he exploits Othello's inability to read anything at all in Iago's mind, including the basic narrative of infidelity. It is not that Othello cannot intuit that Iago is lying; it is that he cannot even construct for himself the hypothetical narrative of infidelity at which Iago hints. Othello's mindblindness, with respect to Iago's duplicity, implies a related metarepresentational cognitive deficit: intimately linked to episodic memory, metarepresentations are 'agent-specifying source tags', allowing us to keep track of who said what, of the sources of information that are typically taken 'under advisement' until that information is proved to be reliable.[1] It follows from Othello's inability to model Iago's mind that he would not, beyond his uncritical refrain of Iago's honesty, seriously consider the characterological intentions behind that mind.

Whether we call such artlessness a virtue or vice, it is one quality among several that renders Othello strange and 'defective' in the minds of his peers (2.1.229). Iago believes that, when compared to Cassio, Othello lacks 'loveliness in favour, sympathy in years, manners and beauties' (2.1.228–9); as a 'lascivious Moor' (1.1.126), he is a gross outlier, an 'extravagant and wheeling stranger' (1.1.136), Roderigo reminds Brabantio, who is certain that Othello is a 'damn'd' enchanter (1.2.63). Othello, for his part, describes himself to be 'rude' in 'speech' (1.3.82), his perceived barbarisms duly assessed and contextualized by critics; and he is of course too easily convinced of Iago's virtue and honesty.[2]

We can better understand Othello's relative mindblindness if we return briefly to his comments on tranquillity and contentment. In his first elevation of the contented life he attributes peacefulness to the absoluteness he gains from loving Desdemona:

> It gives me wonder great as my content
> To see you here before me: O my soul's joy,
> If after every tempest come such calmness,
> May the winds blow, till they have waken'd death,
> And let the labouring bark climb hills of seas,

Olympus-high, and duck again as low
As hell's from heaven. If it were now to die,
'Twere now to be most happy, for I fear
My soul hath her content so absolute,
That not another comfort, like to this
Succeeds in unknown fate.

(2.1.183–92)

Remember that he has just returned from military battle,
which contextualizes the 'tempest' that Desdemona's calming
presence displaces. On one interpretation, contentment is or
will now be achieved in his private life, and serve as a respite
from the tempestuousness of public duty and military service.
But when he is finally pressed into envy by Iago, Othello seems
to mourn the loss of the contentment that he enjoys in that
very military bustle:

I had been happy if the general camp,
Pioners, and all, had tasted her sweet body,
So I had nothing known: O now forever
Farewell the tranquil mind, farewell content:
Farewell the plumed troops, and the big wars,
That makes ambition virtue: O farewell,
Farewell the neighing steed, and the shrill trump,
The spirit-stirring drum, the ear-piercing fife;
The royal banner, and all quality,
Pride, pomp, and circumstance of glorious war!

(3.3.351–60)

How to reconcile this exclamation – which attributes
tranquillity oxymoronically to the pomp and circumstance
of war – with the serenity that he finds with Desdemona?
Perhaps something about the peacefulness that Othello finds
with Desdemona allows him to rationalize his having been
content in war: i.e. she makes him appreciate retrospec-
tively his public persona. This would mean that he deems

Desdemona a reward for public service, or that she makes him a better soldier, or even that war is attractive because he gets to see her afterward (the gist of his earlier comments on tranquillity). Whatever his rationalizations, we can say that he confuses public and private contentment, or draws no fundamental distinction between the two.

Othello only realizes what contentment is for him until he is forced to overthink Desdemona's infidelity. Otherwise he offers sham contentment, the bad faith of someone who would convince himself and us that equanimity reduces to 'success' both on the field and off. This helps us explain some of the odd aspects of his farewell to glory speech. In that speech and related others, war is more of an abstract concept than lived reality for Othello, more about its overall staging and the decorum of preparing for battle than it is combat with relatable others. Even the alleged witchcraft with which he charms Desdemona is populated with the mystified 'Anthrophagi, and men whose heads / Do grow beneath their shoulders' (1.3.144–5), rather than with flesh and blood adversaries. Othello's beloved 'occupation' is to do and act, not to think, not even to acknowledge the basic otherness of anyone with whom he interacts; and this transposes into his relationship with Desdemona, who contributes to his solipsistic absolutism by functioning as the objective trophy wife that critics have often understood her to be for him.

Consider further Othello's notion of contentment in relation to the Stoic/CBT pairing outlined earlier, particularly the Stoic cautioning against taking anything, especially externals, for granted: the wise man does not face psychological reversals because 'foremost in his thoughts [is] the possibility of something obstructing his plans'; and likewise 'every human condition is subject to change', and 'whatever mishap can befall any man can also happen to you'.[3] When Othello expresses 'fear' regarding his soul's imperturbability once united with Desdemona, he worries not that he has become too dependent on her, but that Fortune might never provide something as unassailable: 'For I fear / My soul hath her content so absolute, / That not another comfort, like to this / Succeeds in unknown fate' (2.1.190–3). Othello fears not the loss of tranquillity, but that his current quotient of tranquillity will never admit of increase. He is too present-minded in relishing what he has, and only forward-looking in terms of wanting more.

One of the more recent accounts of embodied cognition, set directly against ToM computationalism, has been described as the 'narrative competency' approach: 'We make sense out of our own actions and out of the actions of others by placing them in a narrative framework.'[4] If ToM abstracts thoughts and behaviour from local circumstances, the narrative approach assumes that we understand ourselves and others in the context of ongoing stories 'in the middle of something that has a beginning and that is going somewhere'.[5] Such stories developmentally require both person-to-person immediacy and autobiographical memory, the upshot being that only when we can formulate a coherent self-narrative are we able to understand others in a narrative way.[6] While some have argued that narrative competency displaces the need for ToM processing, others have proffered a more unitary theory: perhaps in order to understand narrative selves we also need to rely on ToM procedures, either prior or subsequent to the narrative framework; that is to say, in order to access a narrative 'landscape of action', we also need to access a 'landscape of consciousness'.[7]

Particularly interesting, as theorists of narrative selfhood have themselves noted, is the extent to which narrative competency 'may change in certain pathologies'.[8] If we can imagine a version of narrative competency that focuses on the narrator's or subject's salient action and the ambient context, but which features caricatures of people rather than individuals themselves (including their motives, judgements and beliefs), then we have approached 'what it is like' to be Othello. The great irony of Othello's recounting of battle and the military life is that war is distinctly an embodied experience, yet there is little concretely embodied action in his tales. One can imagine that the normal embodied action of such a military life would not only issue in narrative competency, but help one hone one's mind-reading skills. Since contentment for Othello is the placement of himself in an unpeopled, solipsistic narrative, he is unprepared to manage himself and others when forced to acknowledge the problem of other minds. But in order to further contextualize Othello's vulnerable contentment, and link it more directly to his mindblindness, we need to establish his equally complex relationship to cruelty.

Othello puts cruelty first

Assuming that Othello is a touchstone in the play for everything anathema to early modern European values, we might ask, prior to the last act, why he is not demonized as cruel – something we might expect, given that cruelty during the period is repeatedly linked to barbarism. By his own testimony, he has survived the cruelty of others during his military successes. He regales Desdemona with tales of his ability to survive 'Cannibals, that each other eat' (1.3.143). If cruelty presupposes mind-awareness, and the strange and alien Othello is so patently mindblind, it makes sense that he would be a stranger to cruelty itself.

How, though, can we explain the curious turn in the play, namely, that the least cruel character initially turns out to be the only character who owns the cruelty of which he eventually becomes capable? 'Cruel' and its cognates are used four times in the play, three instances of which describe Othello's actions, the last a promise of the cruelty that awaits Iago. Othello's self-avowed cruelty frames his murder of Desdemona. After the third kiss, just before Desdemona awakes, he remarks: 'So sweet was ne'er so fatal: I must weep, / But they are cruel tears; this sorrow's heavenly, / It strikes where it does love' (5.2.20–2). And just after he has attempted to smother Desdemona, alert to her stirring, he exclaims:

What voice is this? Not dead? not yet quite dead?
I that am cruel, am yet merciful,
I would not have thee linger in thy pain, ...
So, so.

(5.2.87–90)

If cruelty is predicated on a ToM, then Othello's discovery of his own cruelty should be contingent on his attribution of a ToM to Desdemona. Othello's baseless notion that Desdemona is full of duplicity suggests that he ascribes to her too robust a mental world, as if he were overcompensating for attributing to Iago too thin a mental fabric (Othello's refrain of Iago's honesty implies that, for Othello, Iago might as well be a two-dimensional embodiment of a discrete virtue). If Othello is too mindblind when it comes to Iago – he begs Iago to 'show' him his thoughts – he veers in the opposite direction of obsessive mind-reading (doubling with Iago) when he finally confronts Desdemona.

But if Othello's ascription of a complex mental world to Desdemona explains his assignation of cruelty to himself, it does not explain why he does so in a Christian context, invoking as he does 'heavenly' sorrow (5.2.21) and then pledging to temper his cruelty with mercy. One way of thinking about divine cruelty as against human cruelty is that the former is the obverse of, even antidote to, the latter. When God acts cruelly he does so to the deserving; cruelty is bound up with retributive justice, however impenetrable the immediate designs of such a *Deus absconditus* might seem. Human cruelty is most effective when it is meted out to the undeserved (which helps to explain why cruelty to animals and children is an especially heinous form). Othello intuits this much when, in his final expostulation with Desdemona before her murder, he compares her treatment of him to being afflicted by God:

Had it pleas'd heaven
To try me with affliction, had he rain'd

All kinds of sores and shames on my bare head,
Steep'd me in poverty, to the very lips,
Given to captivity me and my hopes,
I should have found in some part of my soul
A drop of patience; but, alas, to make me
The fixed figure, for the time of scorn
To point his slow unmoving fingers at ... oh, oh.
Yet could I bear that too, well, very well:
But there, where I have garner'd up my heart,
Where either I must live, or bear no life,
The fountain, from the which my current runs,
Or else dries up, to be discarded thence,
Or keep it as a cistern, for foul toads
To knot and gender in!

                                        (4.2.49–63)

Othello could bear afflictions (read here as heaven's cruelty), but what Desdemona has done to him is beyond cruelty's pale. When he arrogates the office of divine cruelty to himself, he ranges licit cruelty against illicit cruelty. Yet when he stages such a drama he does so still with no complex theory of (God's) mind. As cognitive theorists of religion have suggested, one reason we anthropomorphize is because we tend naturally to attribute a ToM to anything that exhibits external agency: 'We automatically and involuntarily perceive the world as alive and *Person*-like, interpreting even the faintest cues in terms of human traits. That anthropomorphism is so often mistaken does not negate its role or power as the fundamental default assumption.'[9] Othello's God is nothing more than the generic heavens, which might be explicable given that the pagan Moor would not pray to anything like an accommodated or anthropomorphized Christian deity. Yet given Othello's clear conception of the Christian notion of justice tempered with mercy, it would seem that his generic use of the heavens corresponds to his mindblindness coupled with his metarepresentational impairment: heaven is a mysterious (unsourced) but effective retributive agent, the power of which he appropriates when murdering Desdemona.

We might pause here to integrate this manifestation of mindblindness with Othello's vulnerable, manifestly un-Stoic, contentment described earlier. Not to see 'faces in the clouds', not to ascribe particularized agency and intentionality to external events – whether governed by Fortune, God, or nature – underscores Othello's present-mindedness, his incautiousness when contemplating the extent to which his 'possessions' (psychic or otherwise) are vulnerable to future reversals. But this also might be seen as a manifestation (and hence symptom) of Othello's inability to ascribe metarepresentational agency to other human beings: his inability even to attempt to track the agency of Fortune is of a piece with his inability to anticipate the agency of someone like Iago.

But this assumes an asymmetry between Othello's cognizance (however faulty) of Desdemona's secret machinations, and the way in which his cruelty toward her is mitigated for being Christianized: we seem to have an excess of mentalizing in the recipient of cruelty (Desdemona), but a deficiency in the agent of cruelty (Othello). Othello's very staging of cruelty serves to blunt cruelty's effects. At the moment Othello can be cruel, at the moment he believes he has access to all of Desdemona's misperceived manoeuvrings, he opts for a Christian rather than secular notion of cruelty. For Othello to have a personalized or anthropomorphic God dispense punishment would be to implicate himself in the circuit of cruelty by which he himself has been victimized by Iago. If Iago is a 'cruel but merciless God' to Othello, then Othello is a cruel but merciful God to Desdemona. If this is the only form of cruelty of which Othello is capable, it makes sense that Othello does not seem especially concerned with dispensing cruelty toward Iago.

Othello's final gestures toward mitigating cruelty's effects are as staged and romantically overblown as Iago's secret tragedy has been all along. Mindblindness is of a piece with Othello's romantic notion of himself, and it is his lack of empathy born of his mindblindness that explains his staging of cruelty's undoing and 'pluming' of his own will by the play's end. As T. S. Eliot concludes, 'Othello succeeds in turning himself into a pathetic figure, by adopting an aesthetic rather than moral attitude, dramatizing himself against his environment. He takes in the spectator, but the human motive is primarily to take in himself.'[10] I would underscore, against Stanley Cavell's influential reading of the play, that Othello's solipsism or extreme scepticism, fuelled by his mindblindness, is what allows him to imagine that he 'sacrifices' Desdemona. Cavell argues that Othello's exaltation of Desdemona, his 'placing of a finite woman in the place of God', serves as a bulwark against Cartesian scepticism (to render Desdemona a perfect match with Othello is to render his existence secure, invulnerable to existential doubt).[11] It is not Iago's rumours, but Othello's physical and psychological acceptance of Desdemona, her very creatureliness, that renders him sceptical in fostering 'the premonition of the existence of another, hence of his own, his own as dependent, as partial'.[12] Cavell reasons that when Othello sacrifices Desdemona, he compensates by putting himself in her place as God. But rather than say that Othello puts sacrifice to use as an antidote to scepticism, I would say that Othello puts scepticism to use in order to justify sacrifice. Othello does not passively move in and out of sceptical paralysis; rather, his context-sensitive mindblindness fortifies him against such sceptical despair. It is Othello, too, not simply Iago, whose improvisational, defensive skills are subtly displayed for us. He is a character who cannily turns his metarepresentational blunders into rationalized virtue.

Throughout his ruminations leading up to and following his murder of Desdemona, Othello renders both himself and Desdemona fit abstractions. 'It is the cause, it is the cause, my soul, / Let me not name it to you, you chaste stars,' (5.2.1–2) he mutters in preparation for her murder, a quizzical comment that irritated Samuel Johnson: 'The abruptness of this soliloquy makes it obscure. The meaning, I think, is this. "I am here," says Othello in his mind, overwhelmed with horror. What is the reason of this perturbation? ... It is not the action that shocks me, but it is the cause.'[13] To refuse to isolate the cause is to refuse to attribute agency to anything or any person regarding why he has reached this point. He has fashioned himself into generic 'justice' as a filter for the faint empathy that he gives voice to but does not genuinely experience: 'A balmy breath, that doth almost persuade / Justice herself to break her sword' (5.2.16–17). Remember that he has already assured us that he has turned his heart to stone, in keeping with his invocation of 'marble heaven' (3.3.467), which makes his reiteration of the theme nearly redundant when he exclaims to the pleading Desdemona: 'O perjur'd woman, thou dost stone thy heart, / And makest me call what I intend to do / A murder, which I thought a sacrifice' (5.2.63–6). This too puzzled Johnson, who used the elder quarto, but realized that Q1 opts for 'my' instead of 'thy', which allowed Johnson to import a Hamletesque interpretation according to which Desdemona will be 'murdered' without the chance of atonement that would have preceded a proper sacrifice. However we read the pronoun, we cannot take seriously Othello's sense of himself as murderer rather than sacrificer because he unrelentingly soldiers forth, ignoring Desdemona's petition for one death-bed prayer: 'But half an hour, but while I say one prayer!' (5.2.83). He is not denying to Desdemona her sacrificial status by acting with dispatch; he is denying to himself any pause that would allow a reflective and empathetic moment to ensue. From the beginning of the scene (in which he obfuscates to himself the reason why he is at her bedchamber) to the moment of her death (which escapes even a moment's pause for reflection) he has acted like a mindless avenger.

In the aftermath, Othello becomes more, not less mindless, echoing soldierly platitudes as he focuses more on swordplay and wordplay than his own cruelty. Othello has lost his sword to a 'puny whipster' (5.2.245) and then speaks yet another abstraction: 'But why should honour outlive honesty?' (5.2.246), placing himself in a stark morality play in which, presumably, he and Desdemona instantiate the respective virtues of 'honour' and 'honesty'. It is up to Emilia to keep things human, for she will sing longingly to Desdemona and then remind us and Othello of the basics that he has taken for granted: 'Moor, she was chaste, she lov'd thee, cruel Moor' (5.2.250). Never has the most generic of professions, 'She loved thee', made someone so uniquely human, given the dehumanizing context that has prevailed up to this point.

Othello, however, will continue to displace Desdemona and his remorse on to soldierly paraphernalia, eulogizing his Spanish sword when addressing Gratiano: 'Behold, I have a weapon, / A better never did itself sustain / Upon a soldier's thigh: I have seen the day, / That with this little arm, and this good sword, / I have made my way through more impediments / Than twenty times your stop' (5.2.260–5). But then he catches himself, and comes to something like an *anagnorisis*: 'But O vain boast, / Who can control his fate? ... Here is my journey's end, here is my butt / And very sea-mark of my utmost sail' (5.2.265–9). If this is catharsis, it is Othello's final acknowledgement of the Stoic principle of not being able to control one's fate. Yet it has nothing directly to do with Desdemona, who has faded momentarily during his honorific farewell to the warfaring life. His final turn to Desdemona is a last retreat into mindblindness, but with phenomenological bad faith: 'Now: how dost thou look now? O ill-starr'd wench, / Pale as thy smock ... Cold, cold, my girl, / Even like thy chastity' (5.2.273–7). Othello looks (and sees) Desdemona, and then touches her. But in doing so he seems to render her even further from his mind. At a loss for high-flown language, he provides a stock appraisal: Desdemona is 'pale' and 'cold', as pale and cold as any dead body would look and touch to him. He then collects himself, asserts his status oxymoronically as 'honourable murderer' (5.2.295) and spills forth his *apologia* to the state for his traductions (5.2.340–57). Inserted between these speeches is Iago's infamous 'from this time forth I never will speak word' (5.2.305). Against Othello's outsized detachment from himself and his dead wife, Iago's silence uncannily approaches the human.

Ethics and extended cognition: The invulnerability of Othello's mind

But there might be a way to argue that a fuller, more situated cognitive approach can provide Othello a countermanding ethical release and even tragic sublimity. To what extent does Othello rely on extended cognition, and what might be the ethical implications of such scaffolded agency? Consider the conversation that ensues between Othello and Iago after Iago poses the pregnant question, 'Did Michael Cassio, when you woo'd my lady, / Know of your love' (3.3.95–6)? In the span of only 50 or so lines 'think' and its various cognates, including 'thinkings', 'thought', 'thoughts', and 'think'st' appear ten times. When Othello asks why Iago queries him about Cassio, Iago responds, 'for a satisfaction of my thought' (3.3.98), to which Othello counters,'Why of thy thought, Iago?' (3.3.99). After further wordplay, Othello asks again: 'What dost thou think?' (3.3.108) to which Iago responds, 'Think, my lord?' (3.3.109), rejoined by Othello's exasperated: 'Think, my lord? By heaven, he echoes me, / As if there were some monster in his thought' (3.3.110–11), after which he demands: 'Show me thy thought' (3.3.120). The volley protracts tediously – Iago continuing to claim the privacy of his thoughts, even as he divulges them to Othello, Othello plying Iago for more information until he denies that he will play the cuckold without further proof. The exchange asks us to meditate not simply on the generic problem of other minds (Othello is desperate to see, know, and possess Iago's dilations), but on Othello's inability to draw his own inferences regarding the content and vehicle of Iago's thoughts. Othello denies as much, of course: 'Exchange me for a goat, / When I shall turn the business of my soul / To such exsufflicate and blown surmises, / Matching thy inference' (3.3.184–7). But he is well on his way to exchanging his soul for such inferences, despite his resolution to see before doubting. Iago observes that he has agitated Othello – 'I see this hath a little dash'd your spirits' (3.3.219) – and then Othello himself, upon Iago's departure, wonders 'Why did I marry?' (3.3.246), adding that honest Iago 'sees and knows more, much more, than he unfolds' (3.3.246).

If Iago's mind-reading puts him one step before his inter-locutors, Othello's mindblindness puts him one step behind. Rather than mark his own inferences as the conversation unfolds, he allows Iago to draw connections on his behalf. Relinquishing his ability to think on his own to his ensign, Othello's exaggerated avowal that he is 'bound to Iago forever', suggests that, without much scrutiny, he will *own* whatever further information Iago will share on the matter of Cassio and Desdemona. He credits Iago not simply because of Iago's seeming honesty, but because he reasons that Iago has a better mind than he does: 'This fellow's of exceeding honesty, / And knows all qualities, with a learned spirit, / Of human dealing' (3.3.262–4). Eventually, Iago does become a veritable extension of Othello's mind. Consider their otherwise minor exchange regarding the handkerchief just before Othello's first trance. Iago has been needling Othello on the issue of Desdemona's honour, then makes mention of the handker-chief – 'Her honour is an essence that's not seen, / They have it very oft that have it not: / But for the handkerchief' – (4.1.16–18), to which Othello responds: 'By heaven, I would most gladly have forgot it: / Thou said'st (O, it comes o'er my memory, / As doth the raven o'er the infected house' (4.1.19–21). As an infectious house, Othello cannot properly store and retrieve the fateful information that has come into his possession. Like Otto whose faulty memory is enhanced by his notebook, Othello's memory, not simply his ability to infer, deduce, gather evidence, now *includes* Iago. The metaphor of 'infection' works two ways: Iago has of course infected Othello's mind at the outset, but that mind so infected now parasitically relies on Iago's if it is to function at all on its own. Othello even begins to repeat language spoken by and about Iago: when he reproaches Desdemona for shaming him, he worries that he cannot find a place in his soul for a 'drop of patience', miming Iago's repeated caution to show patience; that same scene closes with Othello's reference to 'money for your pains', echoing Iago's 'money for your purse' promise to Roderigo.

Cognitive theorists who support the hypothesis of extended cognition have begun to consider the ethical implications of such environmental scaffolding: 'Can extended entities,' one philosopher asks, 'be moral agents and bear responsibility for actions, in addition to or in place of the individuals typically held responsible? What does it mean to be "autonomous" when one's cognition is influenced and supported by a milieu of environmental factors?'[14] At issue here is the question of the reasonable boundaries of cognitive extension. According to Andy Clark's parity principle of functional equivalence, cognitive extensions ought to meet 'trust and glue' require-ments: external aids need to be used 'habitually, fluently, and transparently', and should be sanctioned by or owned by the responsible cognizers.[15] What is honest Iago if not Othello's 'trust and glue' throughout the play? Othello's very language toward the end seems to realize the strange imbrications of his mind with Iago's. He asks why Iago has 'ensnar'd' his 'soul and body', (5.2.303); then, in his final speech, in which he notes that he loved wisely, remarks that he had not been one 'easily jealous' until he was 'wrought' upon and 'perplex'd in the extreme' (5.2.346–7). Othello is on to something here: his mind was not simply biased or moved to jealousy by a third party; his thinking had become entangled with Iago's mind such that he lost any sense of cognitive boundary and the ability to adjudicate information on his own. This might excuse guilt in his own mind, even if it does not so extenuate his actions to his auditors and the extra-diegetic audience. Iago seems to have the better argument, his final words exploiting our cogni-tivist sense that he functions as an extension of Othello's own thinking: 'I told him what I thought, and told no more / Than what he found himself was apt and true' (5.2.177–8). This means, ostensibly, that Othello had heard what he wanted to hear; but, more suggestively, that, once the cuckolding had begun, Iago had told Othello what he was already thinking; i.e. he served to extend a willing soul rather than corrupt an unwilling one. Even so, a readiness to listen seems to be the only measure of cognitive willpower that Othello exercises in the play. Perhaps the most we can say is that the play leaves provocatively open questions of moral accountability when one prostheticizes one's mind so recklessly in the manner of Othello.

But what, finally, of Othello's tragic dimension? I have already remarked that, in place of ToM attunement, Othello relies on an impossibly disembodied form of narrative selfhood. His strangely unpeopled narratives provide him with the contentment that is threatened by any measure of 'in the head' cognition that he would encounter in himself and others. It's as if his military travails, or at least the narratives thereof, ironically provide him with an escape from intentional thinking. (We have to imagine that Othello's military success hails from an unchecked will and quest for valour, rather than from a fine-grained sifting of his adversaries' intentions and motives; as military *strategist*, Iago would complement Othello handsomely). There is something poignant, if not roundly tragic, about Othello's dilemma: caught between the need and the inability to read other minds, he overextends his thinking to the very individual who serves not simply as a confidence man, but as a prosthetic with a vengeance.

We might say that thinking happens to Othello, rather than that he thinks himself into trouble. He is not just 'acted upon', as Harry Levin remarks, but *thought* upon.[16] Because he faces an encounter with the neural sublime that is embodied in Iago (an encounter with a determinate structure by which his agency is compromised), there is some tragic effect in his downfall. But that tragic quality is offset by a failure of *anagnorisis*. To render himself and Desdemona abstractions, to resuscitate a narrativized martial self that displaces his guilt, to excuse his own cognitive underloading, transferring his thinking to Iago, and then mystifying the entire process: these rationalizations diminish his own and our catharsis. Indeed, it is open to question whether we can even empathize with a character who, by the end of the play, has so withdrawn into his own narrative fictions that he seems unable to empathize with anyone else. If the phenomenological–enactive view of empathy assumes that seeing oneself from another perspective is a basic requirement for selfhood, then, on that robust account, Othello is less a characterological subject than is Iago. While both are alienated from any empathetic, inter-subjective relations, Iago at least displays a rarefied form of 'cognitive empathy' that allows us the critical perspective-taking that tragic identification would seem to require. We do not know what it is like to be Othello at the end of the play, because he has no idea what it is like to be himself.

* * *

Despite the fact, then, that Othello's fate has been neatly packaged for us by the close of the play, and that Iago's fate remains unsettled, tragic catharsis still seems more Iago's than Othello's. Some of us might counterfactually ponder Othello's demise. What if he had not turned to suicide and instead had murdered Iago? Would that have been more or less cathartic for him and for us? But as soon as we muse over Othello's possible worlds, we are brought back to Iago and the more interesting question of the nature of Iago's uncertain fate which, by the close of the play, keeps us suspended despite the psychic closure that it provides him. That the question of Iago's fuller biography exercises our imagination is testified, for example, by the recent publication of two popular novels that attempt to extend his life beyond the boundaries of the play's text. Nicole Galland's *I, Iago* is a prequel that recon-structs Iago's traumatic childhood before the play opens; David Snodin's *Iago* is a sequel that imagines the Cypriotic turmoil that ensues after Iago escapes from prison following the events that close the play.[17] No mere hunting for Iago's motives, these two novels serve the purpose of reconstructing Iago's fuller biography, putting the latter in the service of the former (the unspoken premise of both works is that we can better understand Shakespeare's Iago once we extend in both directions his diachronic, narrative self). The alternative or possible lives of Othello, I submit, invite much less speculation not because of suicidal closure, but because his self-proclaimed biographical and narrative excesses do not suggest the depth of psychic remainder that we intuit in Iago's biographical and narrative silences. While Othello loses cathartic stature in proportion to his own projection of his intentions and motives, Iago acquires cathartic stature in proportion to our ongoing projection of intentionality on to him. Each time that we recreate Iago's sublimely cognitive world, we reveal our own inability to retreat from the very neural sublime that he puts quietly to rest at the end of his own play. I emphasize, finally, that in such re-imaginings of Iago, we likewise project on to him the catharsis that, as obsessive interpreters of his motives, we do not enjoy ourselves.

NOTES

Introduction

1 Thomas Nagel, 'What is it Like to Be a Bat?', *The Nature of Consciousness: Philosophical Debates*, Ned Block, Owen Flanagan and Güven Güzeldere (eds) (Cambridge, MA and London, 1997).

2 For a recent discussion of the easy versus hard problems of consciousness, the latter having to do with the problem of 'experience', in particular, see David J. Chalmers, *The Character of Consciousness* (Oxford, 2010), Chapter 1, *passim*.

3 On conscious inessentialism see Owen Flanagan, *Consciousness Reconsidered* (Cambridge, MA and London, 1992, 5–13).

4 On new mysterianism and anticonstructive naturalism, see Colin McGinn, *The Problem of Consciousness* (Oxford, 1991).

5 Evan Thompson, *Mind in Life: Biology, Phenomenology, and the Sciences of Mind* (Cambridge and London, 2007), 10–15. For a foundational account of enactivism, see Francisco J. Varela, Evan Thompson and Eleanor Rosch, *The Embodied Mind: Cognitive Science and Human Experience* (Cambridge and London, 1993), Chapter 8, *passim*. See also the collected essays in *Enaction: Toward a New Paradigm for Cognitive Science*, John Steward, Olivier Gapenne, and Ezequiel A. Di Paolo (eds) (Cambridge, MA and London, 2010).

6 Samuel Taylor Coleridge, 'Notes and Lectures upon Shakespeare', in *Othello: Critical Essays*, Susan Snyder (ed.) (New York and London, 1988), 9.

7 William Hazlitt, 'Mr. Kean's Iago', *Othello: Critical Essays*, 16.

8 A. C. Bradley, *Shakespearean Tragedy* (New York, 1969), 178–80.

9 G. Wilson Knight, *The Wheel of Fire: Interpretation of Shakespeare's Tragedy* (Cleveland and New York, 1964), 116.

10 Hazlitt, 'Mr. Kean's Iago', 24.

11 Here and throughout the book I use 'intentionality' to describe the manner in which we routinely ascribe propositional attitudes (beliefs, desires, judgements, etc.) to others. For more on intentionality, see Daniel C. Dennett, *The Intentional Stance* (Cambridge, MA and London, 1990).

12 D. Braddon-Mitchell and F. Jackson, *Philosophy of Mind and Cognition* (Oxford, 2007), 129. Cited in *Cognitive Phenomenology*, Tim Bayne and Michelle Montague (eds) (Oxford, 2011), 2.

13 T. Horgan and J. Tienson, 'The Intentionality of Phenomenology and the Phenomenology of Intentionality', *Philosophy of Mind: Classical and Contemporary Readings*, D. J. Chalmers (ed.) (Oxford, 2002), 522. Cited in *Cognitive Phenomenology*, 4.

14 Alan Richardson, *The Neural Sublime: Cognitive Theories and Romantic Texts* (Baltimore, 2010), 37.

15 Ibid., 27–30.

16 Ibid., 35.

17 Ibid., 37.

18 Edward Pechter, '"Iago's Theory of Mind": A Response to Paul Cefalu', *Shakespeare Quarterly*, 64 (2013).

19 Andy Clark and David J. Chalmers, 'The Extended Mind', *The Extended Mind*, Richard Menary (ed.) (Cambridge and London, 2010), 33–7.

20 Blakey Vermeule, *Why Do We Care about Literary Characters?* (Baltimore, 2010), 14.

21 Ibid.

22 Dorrit Cohn, *The Distinction of Fiction* (Baltimore, 1999), 23. Cited in Vermeule, *Why Do We Care about Literary Characters?*, 14.

23 For a critique of phenomenology from a Freudian vantage point, see Paul Ricoeur, *Freud and Philosophy: An Essay on Interpretation*, trans. Denis Savage (New Haven and London, 1970), 390–420. On the use of phenomenology by cognitive theorists, see Flanagan, *Consciousness Reconsidered*, Chapter 8,

passim. The 'horizons of compatibility' between phenomenology and psychoanalysis are the subject of some recent important work, particularly in anthropology. See, for example, C. Jason Throop, 'On Inaccessibility and Vulnerability: Some Horizons of Compatibility Between Phenomenology and Psychoanalysis', *Ethos*, 40 (75–96); and Thomas J. Csordas, 'Psychoanalysis and Phenomenology', *Ethos*, 40 (54–74), particularly pp. 56–7, where Csordas points out that, despite their congruences, reflective phenomenology aims primarily at description, while psychoanalysis is oriented toward therapy.

24 Daniel C. Dennett, 'Who's On First? Heterophenomenology Explained', *Journal of Consciousness Studies*, 10 (2003), 2–12. In its historical variants, put to insightful use by early modernists, phenomenology can provide the contexts in which Iago idiosyncratically thinks: certainly knowledge of Stoic theories of the will and reason, or humoural accounts of the emotions, can help us reconstruct the manner in which early modern audiences understood his locally embedded world. Still, given Iago's intractable self-deceptions, and our abiding sense that there is always so much more to him than what he lets on, phenomenological bracketing will leave us wanting more information about the reasons for his seemingly unaccountable actions. And Iago's peculiar sense of disembodiment itself helps to render him intractable to versions of phenomenology or enactivism that would focus primarily on embodied subjectivity.

25 For an account of the use of ToM to understand intentionality in storyworlds, see Alan Palmer, 'Storyworlds and Groups', in *Introduction to Cognitive Cultural Studies*, 176–92. I use the terms 'phylogenetic' and 'ontogenetic' in keeping with the cognitivist (rather than Freudian) use of these terms in ToM research. An ontogenetic approach allows us to imagine that fictional characters' ToM capacities are revisable and contingent on their very development within plots: their storyworld embeddedness. An ontogenetic understanding of ToM in fiction warrants a supplementary psychoanalytic approach, since psychoanalytic theory can help explain not only underlying reasons for ToM impairments, but the way in which characters work through those impairments. For an evolutionist defence of the ontogenetic nature of ToM, see Cecilia Heyes, 'Four Routes

of Cognitive Evolution', *Psychological Review*, 110 (2003): 713–27: 'The ontogenetic construction hypothesis suggests that the potential to conceive of, or represent, mental states arises in the course of development through experience of one's own behavior and that of others, including and in conjunction with the mentalistic language of those who have already developed mature theory of mind' (720).

26 William Shakespeare, *Othello*, M. R. Ridley (ed.) (Cambridge and London, 1965). All further citations taken from this Arden 2nd edition.

27 See Pechter, '"Iago's Theory of Mind": A Response to Paul Cefalu', 299; and Richard Raatzsch, *The Apologetics of Evil: The Case of Iago* (Princeton, 2009), 50.

28 G. W. F. Hegel, *Phenomenology of Spirit*, trans. A. V. Miller (Oxford, 1977), 122. On Hegel and Stoicism, see Gordon Braden, *Renaissance Tragedy and the Senecan Tradition* (New Haven and London, 1985), 24.

Chapter one

1 See A. C. Bradley, *Shakespearean Tragedy* (London, 1904), 193n1; and Stephen Greenblatt, *Renaissance Self-Fashioning: From More to Shakespeare* (Chicago, 1980), 235.

2 The foundational essay on ToM is David Premack and Guy Woodruff, 'Does the Chimpanzee Have a Theory of Mind?', *Behavioral and Brain Sciences*, 1 (1978): 515–26. On ToM and mindblindness, see Simon Baron-Cohen, *Mindblindness: An Essay on Autism and Theory of Mind* (Cambridge and London, 1997). A good introductory text on cognition and ToM is Ian Apperly, *Mindreaders: The Cognitive Basis of 'Theory of Mind'* (New York, 2011); on literature, culture and ToM, see Lisa Zunshine, *Why We Read Fiction: Theory of Mind and the Novel* (Columbus, 2006) and Zunshine, 'Lying Bodies of the Enlightenment: Theory of Mind and Cultural Historicism', in *Introduction to Cognitive Cultural Studies*, ed. Zunshine (Baltimore, 2010), 115–33. For a good discussion of the different uses in literary criticism of ToM versus simulation

theory, see Blakey Vermeule, *Why Do We Care about Literary Characters?* (Baltimore, 2010), 21–48. For some recent criticism of ToM, see Ivan Leudar and Alan Costall (eds), *Against Theory of Mind* (London, 2011).

3 On the evolutionarily adaptive quality of ToM, especially as it might be represented in literature, see William Flesch, *Comeuppance: Costly Signaling, Altruistic Punishment, and Other Biological Components of Fiction* (Cambridge and London, 2007), 18. For an overview of ToM from the vantage point of evolutionary psychology, see *The Adapted Mind: Evolutionary Psychology and the Generation of Culture*, Jerome H. Barkow, Leda Cosmides, and John Tooby (eds) (Oxford, 1992), 3–15.

4 On optimal experience and flow, see Mihaly Csikszentmihalyi, *Flow: The Psychology of Optimal Experience* (New York, 2008).

5 Several attempts, mostly by cognitive theorists and philosophers of science, have been made to integrate cognitive psychology and the psychoanalytic process. See, for example, Wilma Bucci, *Psychoanalysis and Cognitive Science: A Multiple Code Theory* (New York, 1997), esp. 36–43, which provides an extensive critique of Freudian metapsychology; *Freud and the Neurosciences: From Brain Research to the Unconscious*, Giselher Guttmann and Inge Scholz-Strasser (eds) (Vienna, 1997); and Louis Cozolino, *The Neuroscience of Psychotherapy: Building and Rebuilding the Human Brain* (New York, 2010).

6 James L. Calderwood, *The Properties of 'Othello'* (Amherst, 1989), 113.

7 F. R. Leavis, 'Diabolic Intellect and the Noble Hero: Or, The Sentimentalist's Othello', in *Othello: Critical Essays*, Susan Snyder (ed.) (New York, 1988), 107, 111.

8 Leavis, 107.

9 See Stanley Cavell, *Disowning Knowledge in Seven Plays of Shakespeare*, rev. edn. (Cambridge, 2003), 25.

10 Janet Adelman, 'Iago's Alter Ego: Race as Projection in *Othello*', *Shakespeare Quarterly*, 48 (1997): 125–44, esp. 127–8. Iago's 'emptiness' is also described in Karl F. Zender, 'The Humiliation of Iago', *Studies in English Literature 1500–1900*, 34 (1994), 323–39, esp. 327–8.

11 Jesse M. Bering, 'The Existential Theory of Mind', *Review of General Psychology*, 6 (2002), 12, quoted in Zunshine (ed.), *Introduction to Cognitive Cultural Studies*, 119.

12 Critical assessments of Iago's paranoia include Martin Wangh's 'Othello: The Tragedy of Iago', *Psychoanalytic Quarterly*, 19 (1950), 202–12; and Gordon Ross Smith, 'Iago the Paranoiac', *American Imago*, 9 (1952), 155–67. See also the review of such approaches in Robert Rogers, 'Endopsychic Drama in *Othello*', *Shakespeare Quarterly*, 20 (1969), 205–15.

13 Flesch, esp, 147–54.

14 G. Wilson Knight, *The Wheel of Fire: Interpretation of Shakespeare's Tragedy* (New York, 1964), 114.

15 Premack and Woodruff, 'Does the Chimpanzee Have a Theory of Mind?,' quoted in Alvin I. Goldman, *Simulating Minds: The Philosophy, Psychology, and Neuroscience of Mindreading* (Oxford, 2006), 10.

16 Goldman, *Simulating Minds*, 4.

17 The second-generation cognitivist assumption that ToM is always situated or embodied does not help to explain Iago's peculiar disembodied cognition, at least with respect to his other-regarding ToM. The literature on embodied cognition is now extensive, but for a good phenomenological critique of ToM and domain specificity, see Shaun Gallagher, 'Understanding Interpersonal Problems in Autism: Interaction Theory as An Alternative to Theory of Mind', *Philosophy, Psychiatry, and Psychology*, 11 (2004), 199–217. According to interaction theory, 'The mind of the other is not entirely hidden or private, but is given and manifest in the other person's embodied comportment' (Gallagher, 204).

18 Zunshine, *Why We Read Fiction*, 40, 18.

19 Brian Boyd, *On the Origin of Stories: Evolution, Cognition, and Fiction* (Cambridge and London, 2009), 85. For Steven Pinker's 'by-product' notion of the evolutionary genesis of art, see *How the Mind Works* (New York, 1997), 528.

20 Zunshine, *Why We Read Fiction*, 20.

21 See A. C. Bradley, *Shakespearean Tragedy: Lectures on Hamlet, Othello, King Lear and Macbeth* (Macmillan, 1971), 189.

22 On the cognitive (rather than Freudian) unconscious, see
Timothy D. Wilson, *Strangers to Ourselves: Discovering the
Adaptive Unconscious* (Cambridge and London, 2002), esp.
59–62, on the non-inferential nature of ToM. Earlier accounts
of the domain-specific, discretely modular, nature of ToM
can be found in Baron-Cohen, *Mindblindness*. For a recent
survey of modularity and ToM, and the alternative hypothesis
that ToM is domain general (and admits of ontogenetic
behavioural conditioning), see Philip Gerrans and Valerie E.
Stone, 'Generous or Parsimonious Cognitive Architecture?
Cognitive Neuroscience and Theory of Mind', *British Journal
of the Philosophy of Science*, 59 (2008), 121–41. See also the
section on evolutionary psychology and ToM in David J. Buller,
*Adapting Minds: Evolutionary Psychology and the Persistent
Quest for Human Nature* (Cambridge and London, 2005),
190–200.

23 For an interpretation of the etiology of obsessive-compulsive
disorder from the vantage point of evolutionary psychology,
see Riadh T. Abed and Karel W. de Pauw, 'An Evolutionary
Hypothesis for Obsessive Compulsive Disorder: A Psychological
Immune System', *Behavioural Neurology*, 11 (1998), 245–50.

24 Shaun Nichols, 'The Mind's "I" and the Theory of Mind's "I":
Introspection and Two Concepts of Self', *Philosophical Topics*,
28 (2000), 171–99, esp. 173.

25 Peter Carruthers, *The Opacity of Mind: An Integrative Theory
of Self-Knowledge* (Oxford, 2011), 1.

26 Ibid., 3.

27 For an influential cognitivist explanation of cruelty, see Victor
Nell, 'Cruelty's Rewards: The Gratifications of Perpetrators and
Spectators', *Behavioral and Brain Sciences*, 29 (2006), 211–57.
G. Randolph Mayes provides a good philosophical account
of cruelty in 'Naturalizing Cruelty', *Biology and Philosophy*,
24 (2009), 21–34. The most incisive survey of cruelty from a
cultural studies perspective is Judith N. Shklar's 'Putting Cruelty
First', in *Ordinary Vices* (Cambridge and London, 1984), 7–44.

28 Giuseppe Verdi and Arigo Boito, *Otello: A Lyric Drama in Four
Acts* (Ulan Press, 2012), 14.

Chapter two

1 Meredith Anne Skura, *The Literary Use of the Psychoanalytic Process* (New Haven, 1981), 225.

2 Kamila Markram and Henry Markram, 'The Intense World Theory – A Unifying Theory of the Neurobiology of Autism', *Frontiers in Human Neuroscience*, 4 (2010), article 224, 1–29, esp. 10.

3 Michael Wai and Niko Tiliopoulos, 'The Affective and Cognitive Empathic Nature of the Dark Triad of Personality', *Personality and Individual Differences*, 52 (2012), 794–9, esp. 794.

4 A foundational text on the 'self-monitoring' techniques of cognitive behavioural therapy is Aaron T. Beck's *Cognitive Therapy and the Emotional Disorders* (New York, 1979); for a more recent survey of the technique, see Michelle G. Craske, *Cognitive Behavioral Therapy* (Washington, DC, 2010).

5 Seneca, 'On the Tranquillity of the Mind', *Dialogues and Essays*, trans. John Davie (Oxford, 2007), 114.

6 Ibid., 117.

7 Ibid., 129.

8 Plutarch, 'On Tranquility of Mind', *Moralia*, Vol. VI, trans. W. C. Helmbold (Cambridge and London, 1939), 181.

9 Seneca, 'On The Tranquility of the Mind', 124.

10 See *Coleridge's Essays & Lectures on Shakespeare & Some Other Old Poets & Dramatists*, Ernest Rhys (ed.) (London, 1909), 169.

11 Ibid., 121.

12 Albert Ellis and C. MacLaren, *Rational Emotive Behavior Therapy: A Therapist's Guide* (California, 2005), 5. Cited in Donald Robertson, *Philosophy of Cognitive-Behavioural Therapy: Stoic Philosophy as Rational and Cognitive Psychotherapy* (London, 2010), 5.

13 Albert Ellis, *Reason and Emotion in Psychotherapy: A Comprehensive Method of Treating Human Disturbances* (New Jersey, 1962), 54. Cited in Robertson, *Philosophy of Cognitive–Behavioural Therapy*, 5.

14 Robertson, *Philosophy of Cognitive–Behavioural Therapy*, 5.

15 A. A. Long, *Epictetus: A Stoic and Socratic Guide to Life* (Oxford, 2002), 1. Cited in Robertson, *Philosophy of Cognitive–Behavioural Therapy*, 9.

16 Ibid., 10.

17 Aaron T. Beck, *Cognitive Therapy and the Emotional Disorders* (New York, 1979), 47–8.

18 Ibid., 213.

19 Some of the language here is borrowed from Beck, *Cognitive Therapy*, 240.

20 On Iago's sadism, see, for example, A. André Glaz, 'Iago or Moral Sadism', *American Imago*, 19 (1962), 323–48.

21 David Pollard, 'Iago's Wound', in *Othello: New Perspectives*, eds Virginia Mason Vaughan and Kent Cartwright (Cranbury, NJ, 1991), 89–96, esp. 92.

22 Pollard, 92.

23 For Freud's 1905 account of the convertibility of sadism and masochism, see *Three Essays on the Theory of Sexuality*, trans. James Strachey (New York, 1962). For his more refined, tripartite account of masochism, see 'The Economic Problem of Masochism', in *The Standard Edition of the Complete Psychological Works of Sigmund Freud*, (ed. and trans.) James Strachey et al., 24 vols. (London, 1953–74), 19, 159–70.

24 Jacques Lacan, *The Seminar, Book XI: The Four Fundamental Concepts of Psychoanalysis*, trans. Alan Sheridan (London, 1977), 186.

25 Bruce Fink, *A Clinical Introduction to Lacanian Psychoanalysis: Theory and Technique* (Cambridge and London, 1997), 187. It should be noted that, although Freud eventually elevated masochism to a primary, even primordial state (linked to *thanatos* or the death drive), Lacan insisted that masochism is secondary to sadism: 'Masochism is a marginal phenomenon and it possesses something almost caricatural that moral inquiry at the end of the nineteenth century has pretty much laid bare.' See *The Seminar of Jacques Lacan, Book VII: The Ethics of Psychoanalysis, 1959–1960*, Jacques-Alain Miller (ed.), trans. Dennis Porter (New York, 1992), 239.

26 The performative and reciprocal aspects of masochism underlie the contractual nature of the sadomasochistic fantasy, a quality that is applied compellingly to Shakespeare's *Merchant of Venice* in Drew Daniel's 'Let me have judgement, and the Jew his will': Melancholy Epistemology and Masochistic Fantasy in *The Merchant of Venice*', *Shakespeare Quarterly*, 61 (2010), 206–34.

27 Fink, *A Clinical Introduction to Lacanian Psychoanalysis: Theory and Technique*, 187.

28 Robert Matz, 'Slander, Renaissance Discourses of Sodomy, and Othello', *ELH* 66 (1999), 261–76, esp. 273.

29 A useful survey of critical positions, some psychoanalytic, on the handkerchief can be found in Lynda E. Boose's 'Othello's Handkerchief: 'The Recognizance and Pledge of Love', in *Othello*, Edward Pechter (ed.) (New York, 2004), 262–74.

30 Deleuze remarks that disavowal is common practice among masochists: 'Fetishism, as defined by the process of disavowal and suspension of belief belongs essentially to masochism ... He [Masoch] does not believe in negating or destroying the world nor in idealizing it: what he does is to disavow and thus to suspend it, in order to secure an ideal which is itself suspended in fantasy.' See Gilles Deleuze, 'Coldness and Cruelty', in *Masochism: "Coldness and Cruelty" by Gilles Deleuze and "Venus in Furs" by Leopold von Sacher-Masoch*, trans. Jean McNeil (New York, 1991), 32–3.

31 Fink, *A Clinical Introduction to Lacanian Psychoanalysis*, 187.

32 The impulse of Iago to disavow and separate from Othello is another way of describing the common critical view of the doubling of the two characters. From a psychomachic point of view, Marjorie Garber provides the most sensible recent account of such doubling in *Shakespeare After All* (New York, 2004), 588–616.

33 Tzachi Zamir, *Double Vision: Moral Philosophy and Shakespearean Drama* (Princeton, 2007), 159.

34 Harold Bloom, *Shakespeare: The Invention of the Human* (New York, 1998), quoted in Barbara A. Schapiro, 'Psychoanalysis and the Problem of Evil: Debating *Othello* in the Classroom', *American Imago*, 60 (2003), 481–99, esp. 486.

35 See Fink, *A Clinical Introduction to Lacanian Psychoanalysis*, 187.

36 Ibid., 189.

37 Sigmund Freud, *Beyond the Pleasure Principle*, (ed. and trans.) James Strachey (New York, 1961), 67.

38 Ibid., 67.

39 Freud does return to masochism and the 'destructive' instinct in *Civilization and Its Discontents*, (ed. and trans.) James Strachey (New York, 1961), 77–8.

40 Treating the psychoanalytic approach as a supplement to a cognitive approach thus avoids the 'imperialism' inherent in psychoanalysis cautioned against by Peter Brooks in 'The Idea of a Psychoanalytic Literary Criticism', *Critical Inquiry*, 13 (1987), 334–48, esp. 336.

41 Albert Ellis and Mike Abrams with Lidia D. Abrams, *Personality Theories: Critical Perspectives* (Sage Publications, 2009), 129.

42 Wilson, *Strangers to Ourselves*, 9.

43 In the same spirit, although arguing for the virtuality of the symbolic unconscious, Žižek asks (regarding Benjamin Libet's notion that unconscious, 'neuronal' processes are the sites of 'free' will): 'What if, prior to our conscious decision, there already was an unconscious decision that triggered the "automatic" neuronal process itself?' See Slavoj Žižek, *Organs without Bodies: Deleuze and Consequences* (New York, 2004), 138.

44 I join Benjamin Paris and others in assuming that, because Shakespeare's principals, especially in the tragedies, are mimetic characterizations, they are amenable to psychoanalytic theorizing. Freudian approaches become problematic when they are too diachronizing, for example, when they ascribe to Hamlet hypothetical infantile Oedipal fantasies turned into symptoms after his father's murder. An early example of this approach is Ernest Jones's belief that Hamlet's delay is caused by his identification with Claudius as the murderer of his father in *Hamlet and Oedipus* (New York, 1976). On the weaknesses of such an approach, see Bernard J. Paris, *Character as a*

Subversive Force in Shakespeare: The History and Roman Plays (Newark, 1991), 21.

45 On Shakespeare's 'fatness' of character, or the presupposition that Shakespearean principals are based on actual persons, see Harry Berger Jr., *Making Trifles of Terrors: Redistributing Complicities in Shakespeare* (Stanford, 1997), 337–9, cited in Michael Bristol, 'Confusing Shakespeare's Characters with Real People: Reflections on Reading in Four Questions', in *Shakespeare and Character: Theory, History, Performance, and Theatrical Persons*, Paul Yachin and Jessica Slights (eds) (Basingstoke, 2009), 20.

46 Vermeule, xii–xiii.

47 Alan Richardson, *The Neural Sublime: Cognitive Theories and Romantic Texts* (Baltimore, 2010), 92. On cognitive misunderstanding and *Macbeth*, see Ellen Spolsky, 'An Embodied View of Misunderstanding in *Macbeth*', *Poetics Today*, 32 (2011), 489–520, esp. 491.

48 Drawing on recent findings in neurolinguistics, Norman N. Holland points out that the irresoluble problem of the realism of literary characters derives from the fact that our brains have 'separate what and where systems', allowing us to intuit what constitutes a literary character, filling in missing details as notes (such as Hamlet's 'big toe'). See 'Hamlet's Big Toe?: Neuropsychology and Literary Character', *PsyArt* (17 October 2012), http://www.psyartjournal.com/article/show/n_holland-hamlets_big_toe (accessed 27 October 2014).

49 Spolsky, 'An Embodied View of Misunderstanding in *Macbeth*', 516.

Chapter three

1 On the *4e* conception of the mind, see Mark Rowland, *The New Science of the Mind: From Extended Mind to Embodied Phenomenology* (Cambridge and London, 2010), 3.

2 Ibid., 67–9.

3 On cognitive embodiment, see Lawrence Shapiro, *The Mind Incarnate* (Cambridge and London, 2004). See also, for a critique

of the embodied view, Robert D. Rupert, *Cognitive Systems and the Extended Mind* (Oxford, 2009), Chapter 11, *passim*.

4 For a recent, spirited defence of sensorimotor enactivism, see Alva Noë, *Out of Our Heads: Why You are Not Your Brain, and Other Lessons from the Biology of Consciousness* (New York, 2009); a more radical anti-representational version of enactivism that argues for enactivism with mental content can be found in Daniel D. Hutto and Erik Myin, *Radicalizing Enactivism: Basic Minds without Content* (Cambridge and London, 2013).

5 Andy Clark and David J. Chalmers, 'The Extended Mind', *The Extended Mind*, Richard Menary (ed.) (Cambridge and London, 2010), 32–3.

6 On functional equivalence and the parity principle, see Andy Clark, 'Memento's Revenge: The Extended Mind, Extended', *The Extended Mind*, Menary (ed.), 44–5.

7 For a discussion of the coupling–constitution fallacy and a critique of the parity principle, see Fred Adams and Ken Aizawa, 'Defending the Bounds of Cognition', *The Extended Mind*, Menary (ed.), 68–99. See also Rupert, *Cognitive Systems and the Extended Mind*, 29–35.

8 Daniel D. Hutto, 'Unprincipled Engagements: Emotional Experience, Expression and Response', *Radical Enactivism: Intentionality, Phenomenology and Narrative: Focus on the Philosophy of Daniel D. Hutto*, R. Menary (ed.) (Amsterdam and Philadelphia, 2006), 32.

9 Richard Gipps, 'Autism and Intersubjectivity: Beyond Cognitivism and the Theory of Mind', *Philosophy, Psychiatry, and Psychology*, 11 (2004), 196.

10 On mirror neurons and empathy, see V. Gallese, 'The "shared manifold" hypothesis: from mirror neurons to empathy', *Journal of Consciousness Studies*, 8, 83–107. For a view of empathy that integrates ToM and the sensorimotor account, see J. Decety and P. L. Jackson, 'The Functional Architecture of Human Empathy', *Behavioral and Cognitive Neuroscience Reviews*, 3, 71–100.

11 Evan Thompson, *Mind in Life: Biology, Phenomenology, and the Sciences of Mind* (Cambridge and London, 2007), 386.

12 Ibid., 393.

13 Ibid., 397.

14 A good account of what constitutes the 'mark of the cognitive' in extended cognition can be found in Shannon Spaulding, 'Overextended Cognition', *Philosophical Psychology*, 25 (2012), 472. See also, Rowlands, *The New Science of the Mind*, Chapter 5, *passim*.

15 Lawrence Shapiro, 'James Bond and the Barking Dog: Evolution and Extended Cognition', *Philosophy of Science*, 77 (2010), 403.

16 John Sutton, 'Exograms and Interdisciplinarity: History, the Extended Mind, and the Civilizing Process', *The Extended Mind*, Menary (ed.), 199.

17 Robert B. Heilman, *Magic in the Web: Action and Language in Othello* (Kentucky, 1956), 83.

Chapter four

1 Edward Pechter, '"Iago's Theory of Mind": A Response to Paul Cefalu', *Shakespeare Quarterly*, 64 (2013), 299.

2 Richard Raatzsch, *The Apologetics of Evil: The Case of Iago* (Princeton, 2009), 46.

3 Ibid., 50.

4 See Jonathan Lear, *Open Minded: Working Out the Logic of the Soul* (Cambridge and London, 1999), 195.

5 Taken from Aristotle, *Politics*, VIII.7.1341b32-42a18, revision of Oxford translation in Jonathan Lear, *Open Minded*, 193.

6 See Lear, *Open Minded*, 195–6.

7 Ibid., 196.

8 A. D. Nuttall, *Why Does Tragedy Give Pleasure?* (Oxford, 1996), 36.

9 See Raatsch, *The Apologetics of Evil*.

10 Søren Kierkegaard, *Either/Or*, Part I, (ed. and trans.) Howard V. Hong and Edna H. Hong (Princeton, 1987), 143–4.

11 Adam Wood, 'Is the Tragic Always the Tragic? Kierkegaard on Antiquity and Modernity in Shakespeare', *The Locus of Tragedy*, Arthur Cools, Thomas Crombez, Rosa Slegers, and Johan Taels (eds) (Boston, 2008), 128.

12 See, for example, Anthony Giddens, *Central Problems in Social Theory: Action, Structure, and Contradiction in Social Analysis* (Berkeley, 1979); and Pierre Bourdieu, *The Logic of Practice*, trans. Richard Nice (Palo Alto, 1990).

13 On egolessness and consciousness, see Owen Flanagan, *Consciousness Reconsidered* (Cambridge and London, 1992), Chapter 9, *passim*. On the relationship between conscious and nonconscious cognition, see Timothy D. Wilson, *Strangers to Ourselves: Discovering the Adapted Unconscious* (Cambridge and London, 2002). For an attempt to integrate conscious willing and mechanistic causation, see Daniel M. Wegner, *The Illusion of Conscious Will* (Cambridge and London, 2002). For a spirited, although not necessarily convincing, defence of the ways in which naturalizing the mind can enhance human dignity, see Antonio Damasio, *Self Comes to Mind: Constructing the Conscious Brain* (New York, 2010), 28–30.

14 G. W. F. Hegel, *Aesthetics: Lectures on Fine Art*, volume II, trans. T. M. Knox, (Oxford, 1975), 1194.

15 On the displacement of dynamic psychology by diagnostic psychiatry, see Allen V. Horwitz, *Creating Mental Illness* (Chicago, 2002), especially Chapters 2 and 3.

16 See Jonathan Lear, *Happiness, Death, and the Remainder of Life* (Cambridge and London, 2000), 72.

17 Ibid., 75–7.

18 Ibid., 76.

19 Ibid., 80.

20 Ibid., 109–10.

21 Ibid., 89.

22 Immanuel Kant, *The Critique of Judgment*, 23.2, trans. Donald W. Crawford, in Crawford, *Kant's Aesthetic Theory* (Madison, 1974), 99. Cited in Iain Boyd Whyte, *Beyond the Finite: The Sublime in Art and Science* (Oxford, 2011), 5.

23 Alan Richardson, *The Neural Sublime: Cognitive Theories and Romantic Texts* (Baltimore, 2010), 25.

24 Ibid., 23. Richardson is quoting Guy Sircello, 'How is a Theory of the Sublime Possible?' *Journal of Aesthetics and Art Criticism*, 51.4, 547.

25 Richardson, *The Neural Sublime*, 23.

26 Ibid., 30.

27 Ibid., 33.

28 Ibid., 35.

29 On Schopenhauer and the tragic sublime, especially regarding the death principle, see Julian Young, *The Philosophy of Tragedy: From Plato to Zizek* (Cambridge, 2013), 162.

30 Arthur Schopenhauer, *The World As Will and Representation*, volume II, trans. E. F. J. Payne (New York, 1958), 433.

31 Ibid., 434.

32 Ibid., volume I,, 205.

33 Ibid. On Schopenhauer and the sublime, see Young, *The Philosophy of Tragedy*, 157–60.

34 Daniel C. Dennett, *Sweet Dreams: Philosophical Obstacles to a Science of Consciousness* (Cambridge and London, 2006), 57.

Chapter five

1 On metarepresentation and fiction, see Zunshine, *Why We Read Fiction*, 50–1.

2 On Othello and barbarism, see Ian Smith, 'Barbarian Errors: Performing Race in Early Modern England', *Shakespeare Quarterly*, 49 (1998), 168–86.

3 Ibid., 131–3.

4 Shaun Gallagher, 'The Narrative Alternative to Theory of Mind', *Radical Enactivism: Intentionality, Phenomenology and Narrative: Focus on the Philosophy of Daniel D. Hutto*, R. Menary (ed.) (Amsterdam and Philadelphia, 2006), 226.

5 Ibid.

6 Ibid., 227.

7 Ibid., 226.

8 Ibid., 228.

9 Todd Tremlin, *Minds and Gods: The Cognitive Foundations of Religion* (Oxford, 2006), 99.

10 T. S. Eliot, 'Shakespeare and the Stoicism of Seneca', in *Selected Essays* (London, 1951), 107–20.

11 Cavell, 126.

12 Cavell, 138. Cavell's argument shares much with Norman Rabkin's contention that Othello, Shakespeare's most Christian protagonist, puts too much faith in Desdemona. See Norman Rabkin, *Shakespeare and the Common Understanding* (New York, 1967), 60–3.

13 Samuel Johnson, 'Shakespeare, the Rules, and *Othello*', from Johnson's 1765 edition of Shakespeare, in William Shakespeare, *Othello*, Edward Pechter (ed.) (New York and London, 2004), 219.

14 Mason Cash, 'Extended Cognition, Personal Responsibility, and Relational Autonomy', *Phenomenology and the Cognitive Sciences*, 9 (2010), 645.

15 Ibid., 651.

16 Harry Levin, *Shakespeare and the Revolution of the Times: Perspectives and Commentaries* (Oxford, 1976), 152.

17 See Nicole Galland, *I, Iago: A Novel* (New York, 2012); and David Snodin, *Iago: A Novel* (New York, 2012).

SELECTED BIBLIOGRAPHY

Adams, Fred and Ken Aizawa, 'Defending the Bounds of Cognition', in Richard Menary (ed.), *The Extended Mind* (Cambridge, MA and London, 2010), 67–80.

Adamson, Jane, *Othello as Tragedy: Some Problems of Judgment and Feeling* (Cambridge, 1980).

Adelman, Janet, 'Iago's Alter Ego: Race as Projection in Othello', *Othello, Shakespeare Quarterly*, 48 (1997), 125–44.

Altman, Joel B., *The Improbability of Othello: Rhetorical Anthropology and Shakespearean Selfhood* (Chicago, 2010).

Apperly, Ian, *Mindreaders: The Cognitive Basis of 'Theory of Mind'* (New York, 2011).

Baron-Cohen, Simon, *Mindblindness: An Essay on Autism and Theory of Mind* (Cambridge, MA and London, 1997).

Bayne, Tim and Michelle Montague (eds), *Cognitive Phenomenology* (Oxford, 2011).

Beck, Aaron T., *Cognitive Therapy and the Emotional Disorders* (New York, 1979).

Boose, Lynda E., 'Othello's Handkerchief: "The Recognizance and Pledge of Love"' in *Othello*, Edward Pechter (ed.) (New York, 2004).

Bourdieu, Pierre, *The Logic of Practice*, trans. Richard Nice (Palo Alto, 1990).

Boyd, Brian, *On the Origin of Stories: Evolution, Cognition, and Fiction* (Cambridge and London, 2009).

Boyd Whyte, Iain and Roald Hoffman, eds, *Beyond the Finite: The Sublime in Art and Science* (Oxford, 2011).

Braden, Gordon, *Renaissance Tragedy and the Senecan Tradition: Anger's Privilege* (New Haven and London, 1985).

Bradley, A. C., *Shakespearean Tragedy* (New York, 1969).

Bucci, Wilma, *Psychoanalysis and Cognitive Science: A Multiple Code Theory* (New York, 1997).

Carruthers, Peter, *The Opacity of Mind: An Integrative Theory of Self-Knowledge* (Oxford, 2011).

Cash, Mason, 'Extended Cognition, Personal Responsibility, and Relational Autonomy', *Phenomenology and the Cognitive Sciences*, 9 (2010), 645–71.

Cavell, Stanley, *Disowning Knowledge in Seven Plays of Shakespeare* (rev. edn., Cambridge, 2003).

Chalmers, David J., *Philosophy of Mind: Classical and Contemporary Readings* (Oxford, 2002).

Clark, Andy, 'Memento's Revenge: The Extended Mind, Extended', in Richard Menary (ed.), *The Extended Mind* (Cambridge, MA and London, 2010).

Clark, Andy and David J. Chalmers, 'The Extended Mind', in Richard Menary (ed.), *The Extended Mind* (Cambridge, MA and London, 2010).

Cohn, Dorrit, *The Distinction of Fiction* (Baltimore, 1999).

Cozolino, Louis J., *The Neuroscience of Psychotherapy: Building and Rebuilding the Human Brain* (New York, 2010).

Damasio, Antonio, *Self Comes to Mind: Constructing the Conscious Brain* (New York, 2010).

Deleuze, Gilles, 'Coldness and Cruelty', in *Masochism: 'Coldness and Cruelty' by Gilles Deleuze and 'Venus in Furs' by Leopold von Sacher-Masoch*, trans. Jean McNeil (New York, 1991).

Dennett, Daniel C., 'Who's On First? Heterophenomenology Explained', *Journal of Consciousness Studies*, 10 (2003), 19–30.

Eliot, T.S., 'Shakespeare and the Stoicism of Seneca', in *Selected Essays* (London, Faber, 1951).

Ellis, Albert, *Reason and Emotion in Psychotherapy: A Comprehensive Method of Treating Human Disturbances* (New Jersey, 1962).

Flanagan, Owen, *Consciousness Reconsidered* (Cambridge, MA and London, 1992).

Flesch, William, *Comeuppance: Costly Signaling, Altruistic Punishment, and Other Biological Components of Fiction* (Cambridge, MA and London, 2007).

Freud, Sigmund, 'The Economic Problem of Masochism' (1924), in *The Standard Edition of the Complete Psychological Works of*

Sigmund Freud, (ed. and trans.) James Strachey, et al. 24 vols (London, 1953–74), 19, 159–70.

—*Beyond the Pleasure Principle*, (ed. and trans.) James Strachey (New York, 1961).

—*Three Essays on the Theory of Sexuality*, (ed. and trans.) James Strachey (New York, 1962).

Gallagher, Shaun, 'Understanding Interpersonal Problems in Autism: Interaction Theory as an Alternative to Theory of Mind', *Philosophy, Psychiatry, and Psychology*, 11 (3) (2004), 199–217.

—'The Narrative Alternative to Theory of Mind', in *Radical Enactivism: Intentionality, Phenomenology and Narrative: Focus on the Philosophy of Daniel D. Hutto*, Richard Menary (ed.) (Amsterdam and Philadelphia, 2006).

Giddens, Anthony, *Central Problems in Social Theory: Action, Structure and Contradiction in Social Analysis* (Berkeley, 1979).

Gipps, Richard, 'Autism and Intersubjectivity: Beyond Cognitivism and the Theory of Mind', *Philosophy, Psychiatry, and Psychology*, 11 (3) (2004), 195–8.

Glaz, A. Andre, 'Iago or Moral Sadism', *American Imago*, 19 (4) (1962), 323–48.

Goldman, Alvin I., *Simulating Minds: The Philosophy, Psychology, and Neuroscience of Mindreading* (Oxford, 2006).

Greenblatt, Stephen, *Renaissance Self-Fashioning: From More to Shakespeare* (Chicago, 1980).

Hazlitt, William, 'Mr. Kean's Iago', in *Othello: Critical Essays*, Susan Snyder (ed.) (New York and London, 1988).

Hegel, G. W. F., *Aesthetics: Lectures on Fine Art*, volume II, trans. T. M. Knox (Oxford, 1975).

—*Phenomenology of Spirit*, trans. A. V. Miller (Oxford, 1977).

Hutto, Daniel D., 'Unprincipled Engagements: Emotional Experience, Expression and Response', in *Radical Enactivism: Intentionality, Phenomenology and Narrative: Focus on the Philosophy of Daniel D. Hutto*, Richard Menary (ed.) (Amsterdam and Philadelphia, 2006).

Hutto, Daniel D. and Erik Myin, *Radicalizing Enactivism: Basic Minds without Content* (Cambridge and London, 2013).

Kierkegaard, Søren, *Either/Or*, Part I, (ed. and trans.) Howard V. Hong and Edna H. Hong (Princeton, 1987).

Knight, G. Wilson, *The Wheel of Fire: Interpretation of Shakespeare's Tragedy* (Cleveland and New York, 1964).

Lacan, Jacques, *The Seminar, Book XI: The Four Fundamental Concepts of Psychoanalysis*, trans. Alan Sheridan (London, 1977).

Lear, Jonathan, *Open Minded: Working Out the Logic of the Soul* (Cambridge and London, 1999).

—*Happiness, Death, and the Remainder of Life* (Cambridge and London, 2000).

Leavis, F. R., 'Diabolic Intellect and the Noble Hero: Or, The Sentimentalist's Othello', in *Othello: Critical Essays*, Susan Snyder (ed.) (New York, 1988).

Leudar, Ivan and Alan Costall (eds), *Against Theory of Mind* (London, 2011).

Levin, Harry, *Shakespeare and the Revolution of the Times: Perspectives and Commentaries* (Oxford, 1976).

Long, A. A., *Epictetus: A Stoic and Socratic Guide to Life* (Oxford, 2002).

Markram, Kamila and Henry Markram, 'The Intense World Theory – A Unifying Theory of the Neurobiology of Autism', *Frontiers in Human Neuroscience*, 4 (2010), 224.

Matz, Robert, 'Slander, Renaissance Discourses of Sodomy, and Othello', *ELH* 66 (1999), 261–76.

McGinn, Colin, *The Problem of Consciousness* (Oxford, 1991).

Menary, Richard (ed.), *The Extended Mind* (Cambridge and London, 2010).

Nagel, Thomas, 'What Is It Like to Be a Bat?', in *The Nature of Consciousness: Philosophical Debates*, Ned Block, Owen Flanagan and Güven Güzeldere (eds) (Cambridge and London, 1997) 597–616.

Nichols, Shaun, 'The Mind's "I" and the Theory of Mind's "I": Introspection and Two Concepts of Self', *Philosophical Topics*, 28 (2) (2000), 171–99.

Noë, Alva, *Out of Our Heads: Why You Are Not Your Brain, and Other Lessons from the Biology of Consciousness* (New York, 2009).

Nuttall, A. D., *Why Does Tragedy Give Pleasure?* (Oxford, 1996).

Paris, Bernard J., *Character as a Subversive Force in Shakespeare: The History and Roman Plays* (Newark, 1991).

Pechter, Edward, '"Iago's Theory of Mind": A Response to Paul Cefalu', *Shakespeare Quarterly*, 64 (2013) 295–300.

Plutarch, 'On Tranquillity of Mind', *Moralia*, vol. VI, trans. W. C. Helmbold (Cambridge and London, 1939).

Premack, David and Guy Woodruff, 'Does the Chimpanzee Have a Theory of Mind?', *Behavioral and Brain Sciences* 1 (1978).

Raatzsch, Richard, *The Apologetics of Evil: The Case of Iago* (Princeton, 2009).

Richardson, Alan, *The Neural Sublime: Cognitive Theories and Romantic Texts* (Baltimore, 2010).

Ricoeur, Paul, *Freud and Philosophy: An Essay on Interpretation*, trans. Denis Savage (New Haven and London, 1970).

Robertson, Donald, *Philosophy of Cognitive–Behavioural Therapy: Stoic Philosophy as Rational and Cognitive Psychotherapy* (London, 2010).

Rowlands, Mark, *The New Science of the Mind: From Extended Mind to Embodied Phenomenology* (Cambridge and London, 2010).

Rupert, Robert D., *Cognitive Systems and the Extended Mind* (Oxford, 2009).

Schopenhauer, Arthur, *The World As Will and Representation*, volumes I–II, trans. E. F. J. Payne (New York, 1958).

Seneca, 'On the Tranquillity of the Mind', *Dialogues and Essays*, trans. John Davie (Oxford, 2009)

Shapiro, Lawrence, 'James Bond and the Barking Dog: Evolution and Extended Cognition', *Philosophy of Science* 77 (2010).

Skura, Meredith Ann, *The Literary Use of the Psychoanalytic Process* (New Haven, 1981).

Smith, Ian, 'Barbarian Errors: Performing Race in Early Modern England', *Shakespeare Quarterly*, 49 (1998).

Spaulding, Shannon, 'Overextended Cognition', *Philosophical Psychology*, 25 (2012), 469–90.

Spolsky, Ellen, 'An Embodied View of Misunderstanding in *Macbeth*', *Poetics Today*, 32 (2011), 489–520.

Steward, John, Olivier Gapenne, and Ezequiel A. Di Paolo (eds), *Enaction: Toward a New Paradigm for Cognitive Science* (Cambridge and London, 2010).

Sutton, John, 'Exograms and Interdisciplinarity: History, the Extended Mind, and the Civilizing Process', in Richard Menary (ed.), *The Extended Mind* (Cambridge and London, 2010), 189–226.

Thompson, Evan, *Mind in Life: Biology, Phenomenology, and the Sciences of Mind* (Cambridge and London, 2007).

Tremlin, Todd, *Minds and Gods: The Cognitive Foundations of Religion* (Oxford, 2006).

Varela, Francisco J., Evan Thompson and Eleanor Rosch, *The Embodied Mind: Cognitive Science and Human Experience* (Cambridge and London, 1993).

Vermeule, Blakey, *Why Do We Care about Literary Characters?* (Baltimore, 2010).

Wai, Michael and Niko Tiliopoulos, 'The Affective and Cognitive Empathic Nature of the Dark Triad of Personality', *Personality and Individual Differences*, 52 (2012).

Wangh, Martin, '*Othello*: The Tragedy of Iago', *Psychoanalytic Quarterly*, 19 (1950).

Wilson, Timothy D., *Strangers to Ourselves: Discovering the Adaptive Unconscious* (Cambridge and London, 2002).

Wood, Adam, 'Is the Tragic Always the Tragic? Kierkegaard on Antiquity and Modernity in Shakespeare', in *The Locus of Tragedy*, Arthur Cools, Thomas Crombez, Rosa Slegers and Johan Taels (eds) (Boston, 2008).

Zamir, Tzachi, *Double Vision: Moral Philosophy & Shakespearean Drama* (Princeton, 2007).

Zunshine, Lisa, *Why We Read Fiction: Theory of Mind and the Novel* (Columbus, 2006).

INDEX